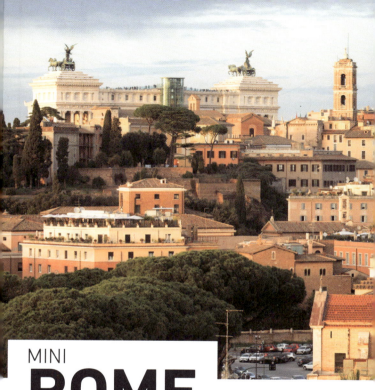

MINI
ROME

YOUR TAILOR-MADE TRIP
STARTS HERE

Tailor-made trips and unique adventures crafted by local experts

HOW ROUGHGUIDES.COM/TRIPS WORKS

STEP 1

Pick your dream destination, tell us what you want and submit an enquiry.

STEP 2

Fill in a short form to tell your local expert about your dream trip and preferences.

STEP 3

Our local expert will craft your tailor-made itinerary. You'll be able to tweak and refine it until you're completely satisfied.

STEP 4

Book online with ease, pack your bags and enjoy the trip! Our local expert will be on hand 24/7 while you're on the road.

PLAN AND BOOK YOUR TRIP AT ROUGHGUIDES.COM/TRIPS

How to download your Free eBook

1. Visit **www.roughguides.com/free-ebook** or scan the **QR code** opposite

2. Enter the code **rome211**

3. Follow the simple step-by-step instructions

For troubleshooting contact: mail@roughguides.com

EAT AND WALK ITALY
COOKING CLASSES

Join our **top-rated cooking classes** in the **heart of Rome!**
Learn how to **make fresh pasta, pizza, tiramisù and more** with **expert chefs**.
Our classes mix **hands on cooking**, helpful tips, and **authentic Italian tradition**, giving you a **true taste of Italy**.
After cooking, **enjoy a meal with the dishes you've made,** in a relaxed and friendly atmosphere in the center of Rome. Perfect for food lovers, solo travelers, couples, families and groups this is your chance to experience **Italy's flavors and culture** up close.

Make your visit to Rome unforgettable!

BOOK NOW!

info@eatandwalkitaly.it   www.eatandwalkitaly.it

Contents

- **6 Introduction**
  - 12 10 Things not to miss
  - 14 A perfect tour of Rome
  - 16 Romantic Rome
  - 18 Unique Rome
- **20 History**
- **33 Places**
  - 33 Piazza Venezia and Capitoline Hill
  - 37 Ancient Rome
  - 47 Centro Storico
  - 57 Spanish Steps and Tridente
  - 62 The Trevi Fountain and Quirinale
  - 66 Villa Borghese
  - 69 The Vatican
  - 81 Trastevere, The Aventine and Testaccio
  - 85 Monti and Esquilino
  - 89 Further afield
  - 93 Excursions
- **99 Things to do**
  - 99 Culture and nightlife
  - 102 Shopping
  - 105 Sports and activities
  - 105 Rome for children
  - 106 Festivals and events
- **108 Food and drink**
- **126 Travel essentials**
- **142 Index**

Introduction

The saying 'all roads lead to Rome' is not just a figure of speech. It is thought that the phrase comes from the fact that the ancient Romans built such an awesome network of roads that all routes did, indeed, radiate from the capital of the Roman Empire. During the time of ancient Rome, which stretches from the founding of the city in the eighth century BC to the collapse of the Roman Empire in the fifth century AD, the Eternal City was seen as the *caput mundi* – 'capital of the world', the base of an empire stretching from Gaul and Spain in the west to Egypt and Asia Minor in the east.

Throughout history, Rome has attracted all kinds of different peoples and engendered many legacies. It was an artistic haven

WHEN TO GO

The European summer is peak season in Italy, but it is also the hottest and busiest time of year. Romans traditionally go on holiday in August – the warmest and most humid month – shutting down their businesses and deserting the city. However, with less traffic, fewer crowds and a great musical programme in the evening, Rome in August has its special charm, and tourists (and residents) are starting to appreciate it more. Rome's low season usually runs from November through March. Though the weather can be cold and rainy, the crowds have either disappeared or haven't arrived yet, the major attractions are easier to access, and prices of airfares and accommodation are lower. For flexible visitors, the shoulder season (April through June and September through October) can be a very pleasant time to visit: the climate is mild, and the city not excessively crowded. Romans call the month of October the *ottobrate Romane*, with its balmy, sunny days and gentle, breezy evenings. Around this time, certain attractions will be at their most beautiful set against the autumnal colour palette.

The iconic Trevi Fountain

during the Renaissance, a sanctuary for well-to-do travellers doing the nineteenth-century 'Grand Tour', and the home of the seat of the Roman Catholic Church from the first Holy Year (1300). Its long and storied history is etched across the stones of its ancient buildings, from classical Roman to Baroque and contemporary, and it is this jigsaw of artistic and architectural styles that makes Rome so breathtakingly unique. No other city in the world represents the different eras of the past two thousand-plus years as well as the Eternal City.

Geographically and psychologically, the city is slightly closer to the laid-back south than to the can-do north of Italy; yet Rome is not a city that stands still. In the 27 centuries of its existence, it has seen empires rise and fall, popes and caesars come and go, and artistic movements flourish and fade. Today, as a modern and

> **ROME IN NUMBERS**
>
> Rome is built on seven hills – Aventine, Capitoline, Caelian, Esquiline, Palatine, Quirinal and Viminale – around the River Tiber, 35km (22 miles) from the sea. The city, the *Comune di Roma*, has a population of about 2.7 million and occupies 1507 square kilometres (582 square miles) including the independent city-state of the Vatican City, which takes up less than half a square kilometre (0.19 square miles).

cosmopolitan European capital, Rome plays the part of a political and business city, while attempting to preserve its unparalleled cultural heritage.

A city that keeps evolving

Visitors may be bowled over by the Italian capital's treasures, but today's Romans take them in their stride. They are accustomed to conducting their daily lives against this awesome backdrop, which means that refreshingly, the city is not treated as a dusty museum piece, but rather a destination in which normal people go about their business.

However, such vibrance and bustle can be destructive to vulnerable historic monuments, which have been impacted by the fumes and constant low vibrations of relentless traffic. But the damage can't be blamed entirely on what's happening on the surface. Geologists have been forced to map the labyrinth of subterranean tunnels far below the streets, which date back to the founding of Rome, as they caused over eighty above-ground structures to collapse.

Tourism, too, has taken its toll on the city. Rome's mayors have all tried to improve travel-related services. Around the year 2000, a programme of public works was devised to restore monuments, archaeological sites and churches. The economic crisis slowed things down, and between 2008 and 2013, Rome's cultural life suffered from severe budget cuts under right-wing mayor Gianni Alemanno. His successor, Ignazio Marino, pedestrianised the Colosseum portion of Via dei Fori Imperiali in 2013 to protect its ancient monuments, reduce traffic pollution and make the area more visitor-friendly.

The anti-establishment Virginia Raggi was elected mayor in 2016 and pledged to 'restore legality and transparency to the city's institutions after twenty years of poor governance'. In 2019 she initiated law changes tackling the 'misbehaviour of tourists', such as jumping into the fountains or bouncing luggage down the steps of ancient sites. When her term ended in 2021, she was succeeded by

Rome is always packed with tourists, particularly in summer

Largo di Torre Argentina

SUSTAINABLE TRAVEL

Traffic pollution has long been a problem in Rome, but over the past decade efforts have been made to redesign urban spaces to promote walking and cycling, which has included expanding the city's network of bike lanes. Nevertheless, there's still a long way to go. Waste management, too, is an issue in the capital. The city is making better strides when it comes to food sustainability. Romans pay a lot of attention to high-quality ingredients that are local and in season, often shopping for organic produce at fruit and veg markets, some of which focus specifically on locally farmed products, such as Campagna Amica on Via di San Teodoro. And while most restaurants offer vegetarian and vegan options, an ever-growing crop of dedicated plant-based eateries are springing up across the city, especially in the centre.

WHAT'S NEW

Rome may be eternal, but that doesn't mean things never change. Over the past four years, preparations for the 2025 Catholic Jubilee have sparked dozens of renovations and building works to make the city more attractive and better facilitate visitor flow. The biggest project was the pedestrianisation of Piazza Pia, which involved the creation of a new walkway between the Vatican and Hadrian's Mausoleum. Elsewhere, restorations were undertaken on the Sant'Angelo Bridge and many fountains, including those at Piazza Navona, the Trevi Fountain, Piazza Farnese, and Piazza di Santa Maria Maggiore. There's a new car-free zone in part of Piazza del Risorgimento, recently added fountains in Piazza San Giovanni, and ongoing construction around the Colosseum and Forum, which is slated to become the world's most important archaeological park. Meanwhile, the city has also been repurposing unused spaces such as old factories and bus depots. In Prati, a former bus park has been transformed into the PratiBus District (www.pratibusdistrict.com), hosting interactive exhibitions, fairs and events, while the erstwhile ATAC San Paolo depot organises regular vintage markets (www.vintagemarketroma.it) and exhibitions.

centre-left Roberto Gualtieri, whose most important task to date is to manage the construction and urban restyling works in view of the 2025 Catholic Jubilee (see box).

Daily life

Visitors need not worry about following the 'when in Rome…' maxim; simply relax and slip into the rhythms of the day and you'll find yourself naturally doing as the Romans do. Instead of toiling around sights in the sweltering afternoon heat, you're much better off joining the locals in the cool shade of Rome's green parks or soaking up the atmosphere in a piazza with a refreshing *grattachecca* (shaved ice with syrup) or perhaps an Aperol spritz.

10 Things not to miss

1. **THE COLOSSEUM**
   The largest ancient amphitheatre ever built. See page 45.

2. **VILLA BORGHESE PARK**
   Home to the excellent Galleria Borghese, the Etruscan Museum and a modern art museum. See page 66.

3. **THE TREVI FOUNTAIN**
   Legend has it that using your right hand to throw a coin over your left shoulder will guarantee a return to Rome. See page 62.

4. **THE SPANISH STEPS**
   The monumental stairway has been a popular meeting place for centuries. See page 58.

5. **VILLA D'ESTE**
   Around 20 miles east of Rome, this sixteenth-century villa has one of Italy's greatest gardens. See page 94.

6. **THE SISTINE CHAPEL**
   The official residence of the pope, the iconic ceiling by Michelangelo is truly awe-inspiring. See page 79.

7. **CAMPO DE' FIORI**
   Rome's colourful open-air market, known for its fruit, vegetables and flowers. See page 54.

8. **THE ROMAN FORUM**
   Imposing ruins mark the hub of the ancient city that ruled a vast empire for centuries. See page 39.

9. **VATICAN CITY**
   The tiny papal state is at the heart of the Catholic church. See page 69.

10. **THE PANTHEON**
    The ceiling of Ancient Rome's best-preserved monument is an astounding feat of engineering. See page 48.

A perfect tour of Rome

9AM

Breakfast. Start your day in Trastevere at *Caffè di Marzio* (Piazza di Santa Maria), where you can savour freshly baked pastries with a view of the pretty square and its centrepiece fountain.

10AM

Janiculum Hill. Take Via Garibaldi to Piazzale Garibaldi at the top of Janiculum Hill for splendid vistas of the city and St Peter's dome. On the way up, veer off towards the San Pietro in Montorio church to peek at Bramante's Tempietto.

11.30AM

Galleries. Head back down through Trastevere's winding streets towards Piazza Trilussa and the Tiber, checking out the independent boutiques and art galleries as you go.

12.30PM

Campo de' Fiori. Cross pedestrian Ponte Sisto and continue up Via Pettinari. Turn left onto Via dei Giubbonari and stop for lunch at picturesque Campo de' Fiori market, where the city's traders have sold their wares for hundreds of years.

1.30PM

Piazza Navona. Cross busy Corso Vittorio Emanuele and stroll along Corso Rinascimento. To the left is the sprawling Piazza Navona, where you'll find Bernini's fountain in the centre. Here you can grab a classy, if pricey, espresso, or a chocolate ice cream *tartufo* at *Tre Scalini*.

2.15PM

Pantheon. To the right of Corso Rinascimento on parallel road Via di Santa Giovanna d'Arco, you'll find the San Luigi dei Francesi church at No. 5. Inside are three of Caravaggio's most famous paintings, including *The Calling of Saint Matthew*. Take Via del Seminario, at the end of which you'll be confronted with the colossal Pantheon.

3PM

Spanish Steps. Walk east along the narrow Via dei Pastini and follow the high-end shopping streets Via del Corso and Via Condotti to Piazza di Spagna. Nose around the Keats-Shelley House at the base of the Spanish Steps, and then head down Via del Babuino to the sculptor Canova's old studio at No. 150, which has been transformed into a café with marble masterpieces tucked in every corner.

5PM

Art in the park. Amble through Villa Borghese Park and check out the contemporary art collection within the Museo Carlo Bilotti.

7.30PM

Dinner. Catch bus #490 or #495 and hop off at the last stop inside the park. Head to *Giano Restaurant* (Via Liguria 28) to feast on fine Sicilian cuisine; book a table in the lovely garden. Later, sip on cocktails at *Doney*, which is as posh today as it was when Federico Fellini immortalised the street in his 1960 classic *La Dolce Vita*.

Romantic Rome

8AM

Caffeine hit. Make an early start with a delicious cappuccino at *Casina del Lago* (Viale dell'Aranciera 2), by the Villa Borghese pond, then take a restorative stroll around the park.

9AM

The art of love. Stake a claim at the front of the queue for Galleria Borghese and marvel at the art that represents love in all its facets, with depictions of Venus and Cupid, tormented love, and romantic legends. See page 67.

11AM

Parco Savello. Take a cab or hire a Vespa for the day (www.vittoriarent.it) and hotfoot it to Parco Savello (Via di Santa Sabina), also known as Giardino degli Aranci. Perched atop Aventino, this hilltop park is one of Rome's most romantic, dotted with orange trees and home to a stunning terrace offering fine views of St Peter's.

NOON

Secret keyhole. A short walk along Via di Santa Sabina takes you to the villa of the Cavalieri di Malta (Knights of Malta). The gate's keyhole offers an astonishing view of St Peter's dome, framed by an avenue of cypress trees. See page 84.

1PM

Sea to plate. Vespa or taxi to Trastevere for lunch at *La Gensola* (Piazza della Gensola 15), a cosy, family-run restaurant that specialises in seafood. The cuisine is exceptional and there's a lovely outdoor patio to take in local life.

2.30PM

Trastevere. Lose yourself in Trastevere's tangle of alleys to stumble across hidden shops, cafés and bars (see page 82). Pick your way to Piazza Santa Maria for an espresso, then press on to Via del Moro, the perfect street for quirky souvenirs such as handmade wooden toys or leather bags. At the end of the road, cross Ponte Sisto for scenic views of the Tiber.

4PM

Shopping. Wander the winding roads that surround the Pantheon, browsing the local shops and independent boutiques along Via di Campo Marzio. Stop for ice cream at *Giolitti* (Via Uffici del Vicario 40); try the fabulous champagne flavour.

6PM

Sundowner. There's nothing like an *aperitivo* at sunset, overlooking the city from the rooftop terrace of *Eitch Borromini* (Via di Santa Maria dell'Anima 30). If you're willing to splurge, stay for dinner and savour the intriguing menu inspired by Roman culinary traditions.

11PM

Throw a coin. Now's the best time to head to the Trevi Fountain and enjoy its splendour without the crowds. Throw in a coin with your beloved to ensure that you'll return to Rome together.

Unique Rome

9AM

Breakfast. Start your day with an Italian breakfast at gorgeously old-fashioned *Antico Caffè della Pace* (Via della Pace 3). Founded in the late 1800s, this historic café was a favoured hangout of artists, directors, actors and intellectuals well into the twentieth century.

10AM

Pasta class. Learn the secrets of Italian cuisine by booking a class with Eatalian Cooks (https://eataliancooks.com), a culinary school near Piazza Navona. Pick between home-made *fettuccine*, gnocchi, pizza and *gelato*. It's a great way to learn a local skill and meet other people.

NOON

Secret courtyard. Walk towards Campo de' Fiori and stop at Via del Pellegrino 19. Peek through the small arched walkway and you'll see the Arco degli Acetari, a medieval courtyard that gives a glimpse of past Roman life. Continue to the plaza and pass through Via dei Giubbonari to reach the Jewish Ghetto.

1PM

Jewish delicacy. In the heart of the Jewish quarter, *Ba'Ghetto* (Via del Portico d'Ottavia 57) is known for its *carciofi alla giudia*, or Jewish-style artichokes. Eating one is an experience in its own right: peel back the petals one at a time, find the soft part and discard the rest, and then use a fork and knife when you reach the heart.

2.30PM

Ancient art and industrial machinery. Cross the river via Tiber Island and take bus #23 to Centrale Montemartini on Via Ostiense. Housed in a former power plant, this unique museum displays ancient Roman statues against a backdrop of industrial machinery – the contrast is stunning. See page 92.

5PM

Artist enclave. Book a cab to the Spanish Steps and enjoy a cup of tea and biscuits from all-English *Babingtons* teahouse (Piazza di Spagna 23), then take a stroll along Via del Babuino and Via Margutta, historically Rome's artist streets, to browse the independent galleries and antique shops.

7PM

Dinner in Canova's atelier. Walk back to Via del Babuino for a one-of-a-kind dining experience at *Canova Tadolini* (Via del Babuino 150/A), the very atelier where sculptor Canova produced some of his most spectacular artworks. The restaurant houses an impressive collection of Neoclassical works and has a refined Italian menu.

8PM

Opera. Book tickets for the Teatro dell'Opera. If you're lucky, they'll be playing Puccini's *Tosca*, set in Rome in the 1800s. In summer, the season moves to Terme di Caracalla, an incredible setting amid the ruins of ancient Rome's baths.

History

Legend claims that Rome was founded by Romulus, who was sired with his twin brother Remus by the god Mars of a vestal virgin and left on the Palatine Hill to be suckled by a she-wolf. Historians date the founding of the city at 753 BC.

Archaeologists have further established that the site was occupied from the Bronze Age, around 1500 BC. By the eighth century BC, villages had sprung up on the Palatine and Aventine hills and, soon after, on the Esquiline and Quirinal ridges. These spots proved favourable since they were easily defensible and lay close to where the River Tiber could be forded. After conquering their neighbours, the Romans merged the villages into a single city and surrounded it with a defensive wall. The marshland below the Capitoline Hill was drained and became the Forum.

The Republic

A revolt by Roman nobles in 510 BC overthrew the last Etruscan king and established the Republic that was to last for the next five centuries. At first the Republic, under the leadership of two patrician consuls, was plagued by confrontations between patrician (aristocratic) and plebeian (popular) factions. Eventually, the plebeians put forward their own leaders, the tribunes, and a solid political order evolved.

In 390 BC, the Gauls besieged the city, destroying everything but the citadel on the Capitoline Hill. When the Gauls left, the hardy citizens set about rebuilding, this time enclosing their city behind a wall of huge tufa blocks. For more than eight centuries, no foreign invader breached those ramparts.

Rome now extended its control to all of Italy, consolidating its hold with six military roads fanning out from the city – Appia, Latina, Salaria, Flaminia, Aurelia and Cassia. By 250 BC, the city's population had grown to 100,000. Victory over Carthage in

Romulus and Remus suckled by a she-wolf

the Punic Wars (264–146 BC) and conquests in Macedonia, Asia Minor, Spain and southern France, expanded Roman power in the Mediterranean. When Hannibal crossed the Alps and invaded Italy in the Second Punic War, large areas of the peninsula were devastated and peasants sought refuge in Rome, swelling the population still further.

The acquisition of largely unsought territories brought new social and economic problems. Unemployment, poor housing and an inadequate public works programme provoked unrest within the city. Civil wars shook the Republic, which ultimately yielded to dictatorship. Julius Caesar, a former proconsul who had achieved some fame by subduing Gaul and Britain, crossed the tiny Rubicon River, which marked the boundary of his province, and marched boldly on Rome to seize power.

Built in the first century AD, the Colosseum could seat 50,000

The Empire

Caesar sought to combat unemployment and ease the tax burden, but his reforms bypassed the Senate and he made dangerous enemies. His assassination on the Ides of March in 44 BC led to civil war and to the despotic rule of his adopted son Octavian, who, as Augustus, became the first emperor (see page 61). Under Augustus, *Pax Romana* – the peace, or rather the rule of Rome – held together the far-flung Empire. To make Rome a worthy capital, he added fine public buildings in the form of baths, theatres and temples, claiming he had "found Rome brick and left it marble". He also introduced public services, including the first fire brigade. This was the Golden Age of Roman letters, distinguished by poets and historians; Horace, Livy, Ovid and Virgil.

In the first centuries of the Empire, tens of thousands of foreigners flooded into Rome, among them the first Christians, including St Peter and St Paul. The emperors tried to suppress this 'new religion', but the steadfastness of its adherents and their willingness to become martyrs increased its appeal.

Each of Augustus' successors contributed his own embellishments to Rome. In the rebuilding after a disastrous fire ravaged the city in AD 64, Nero provided himself with an ostentatious villa, the Domus Aurea (Golden House), on the Esquiline Hill. Hadrian reconstructed the Pantheon, raised a monumental mausoleum for himself (Castel Sant'Angelo), and retired to his magnificent estate, Villa Adriana at Tivoli.

In the late first and second centuries AD, Rome reached its peak, with a population of over one million. Inherent flaws in the imperial system, however, began to weaken the emperor's power and eventually triggered the downfall of the Empire.

After the death of Septimius Severus in AD 211, 25 emperors reigned in just 74 years, many of them assassinated. Fire and plague took their toll on the city's population. In 283 the Forum was almost completely destroyed by fire and never recovered its former magnificence.

After a vision of the Cross appeared to him on a battlefield, the story goes, Emperor Constantine I converted to Christianity. He ensured that Christianity was tolerated by an edict passed in 313, and he built the first churches and basilicas in Rome. In 331 he effectively split the Empire in two when he moved the imperial seat to Byzantium (Constantinople, modern Istanbul). Many of the wealthy, as well as talented artists, joined him and the old capital never recovered.

The fall of Rome

As the Western Empire fell into decline, the Romans recruited northern tribes into the legions to help defend it against other outsiders. But the hired defenders soon deserted, and the disenchanted and weary Roman populace failed to summon up the same enthusiasm to defend the city that they had shown in conquering an empire.

Wave after wave of 'Barbarians' (foreigners) came to sack, rape, murder and pillage; Alaric the Visigoth in 410, Attila the Hun, the Vandals and the Ostrogoths. Finally, the Germanic chief Odoacer forced the last Roman emperor, Romulus Augustulus, to abdicate in 476. The Western Empire had limped to an end, though the

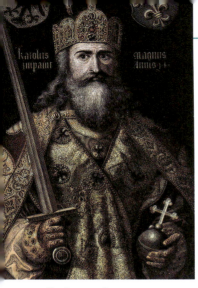

Charlemagne, Roman Emperor from 800 to 814

Eastern Empire continued until 1453.

Papal power

In the sixth century, Justinian re-annexed Italy to the Byzantine Empire and codified Roman law as the state's legal system. But, as later Byzantine emperors lost interest in Rome, a new power arose out of the chaos; the papacy. Pope Leo I (440–61) asserted the Bishop of Rome as Primate of the Western Church, tracing the succession back to St Peter who had been martyred in the city. Pope Gregory the Great (590–604) showed statesmanship in warding off the Lombards, a Germanic tribe already established in the north of Italy. In the eighth century, citing a document, the *Donation of Constantine* (later found to be a forgery), the popes began to claim authority over all of Italy.

Seeking the support of the powerful Franks, Pope Leo III crowned their king, Charlemagne, emperor in St Peter's Basilica on Christmas Day 800. But the Pope in turn had to kneel in allegiance to the Emperor, and this exchange of spiritual blessing for military protection sowed the seeds of future conflict between the papacy and secular rulers.

Over the next four hundred years, Italy witnessed invasions by Saracens and Magyars, Saxons and Normans (who sacked Rome in 1084), with papal Rome struggling along as only one of many feudal city-states on the now-tormented peninsula. The papacy, and with it Rome, was controlled by various powerful families from the landed nobility.

As the situation in Rome degenerated into chaos – deplored by Dante in his *Divine Comedy* – the popes fled in 1309 to comfortable exile in Avignon, and remained under the protection of the French king until 1377. Rome was left to the brutal rule of the Orsini and Colonna families.

The Renaissance

Returning to Rome, the popes harshly squashed any resistance to their rule and remained dominant in the city for the next four hundred years. During the fifteenth and sixteenth centuries, the papacy became a notable patron of the Renaissance, that remarkable effusion of art and intellectual endeavour which transformed medieval Rome from a squalid, crumbling and fever-ridden backwater to one of the foremost cities of the Christian world.

It was Giorgio Vasari, facile artist and first-rate chronicler of this cultural explosion, who dubbed this movement a *rinascita*, or rebirth of the glories of Italy's Greco-Roman past. The father of Rome's High Renaissance, Pope Julius II (1503–13), was responsible for the new St Peter's Basilica. He also commissioned Michelangelo to paint the ceiling of the Sistine Chapel and Raphael to decorate four rooms which are now part of the Vatican Museums, known as the Raphael Rooms (*Stanze di Raffaello*). Donato Bramante, the architect, earned the nickname *maestro ruinante* because of the countless ancient monuments he had dismantled for the Pope's megalomaniacal building plans.

— **NOTES** —

By the eighth century, Rome had been reduced to just a village. Its small population deserted the city entirely when Barbarian invaders cut the imperial aqueducts.

With the treasures uncovered during this process, Julius founded the Vatican's magnificent collection of ancient sculpture.

But the exuberant life of Renaissance Rome was abruptly and brutally extinguished in May 1527 by the arrival of the German troops of Holy Roman Emperor Charles V; the last – and worst – sacking of the city.

In the mid-seventeenth century, Martin Luther, John Calvin and other leaders of the Reformation challenged the papacy and the doctrines of the Church of Rome. A Counter-Reformation was proclaimed in 1563, reinforcing the Holy Office's Inquisition to combat heresy and the Index to censor the arts. Protestants fled and Jews were confined to a ghetto.

Hitler and Mussolini, 1940

Art proved a major instrument of Counter-Reformation propaganda. As the Church regained ground, it replaced the pagan influences of classicism with a more triumphant image, epitomised by Bernini's grand Baroque altar canopy in St Peter's. The Baroque movement flourished in Rome as in no other Italian city.

The Habsburgs

In the eighteenth century, Spain's authority over many of Italy's states passed to the Habsburgs of Austria, who were determined to

Sculpture of Pope Julius II (1503–13), the father of Rome's High Renaissance

curb papal power in Rome. The influential order of Jesuits was dissolved, while Habsburg church reforms meant a crippling loss of revenue and the papacy lost prestige. In 1798 Napoleon's troops entered Rome, later seized the Papal States and proclaimed a Republic. They treated Pius VI with contempt and carted him off to be a virtual prisoner in France. His successor, Pius VII, was forced to proclaim Napoleon as emperor and was also taken prisoner.

During the French occupation, a national self-awareness began to develop among Italians to challenge foreign rule. Many looked to Pope Pius IX to lead a nationalist movement, but he feared the spread of liberalism and when Giuseppe Mazzini set up a Republic in Rome in 1848, the Pope fled. He returned the following year, after the fall of the Republic.

National unity was achieved in 1861 through the shrewd diplomacy of Prime Minister Cavour, the heroics of a guerrilla general, Giuseppe Garibaldi, and the leadership of King Vittorio Emanuele of Piedmont. Rome took over from Florence as capital in 1871 and Pope Pius IX retreated to the Vatican, a 'prisoner of the monarchy'.

The modern era

In World War I, Italy sided with the allies against Austria and Germany. But after the peace conference of 1919, disarray on the political scene sparked an economic crisis, with stagnant productivity, bank closures and rising unemployment. From this turmoil the Fascist movement grew, and when the *fascisti* marched on

Garibaldi monument in Piazza Garibaldi

Rome in 1922, King Vittorio Emanuele III invited their leader, Benito Mussolini (known as *Il Duce*, 'The Leader'), to form a government. Once in power, Mussolini made peace with the Pope through the Lateran Treaty of 1929, which created a separate Vatican State and perpetuated Roman Catholicism as the national religion. In 1940 Mussolini sided with Hitler in World War II, but the Allies declared Rome an open city to spare it from bombing. It was liberated in 1944, intact.

Post-war 'miracle'

The initial post-war period was a time of hardship, but the 1950s saw Rome enjoying Italy's 'economic miracle'. Celebrities made the city their playground, finding *la dolce vita* in the nightspots of the Via Veneto. Rome's population soared, as immigrants from the south came in search of work.

In the 1970s, the city weathered a storm of both left- and right-wing political terrorism, and the decade became known as Italy's *anni di piombo* ('years of lead'), during which the country experienced street fighting, armed combat and terrorism. Perhaps the darkest hour came in 1978 when the Red Brigades, a far-left armed organisation, kidnapped and murdered the former prime minister, Christian Democrat Aldo Moro.

Nowadays, changes are underway to make city services more efficient, and authorities are attempting to tackle pollution and traffic congestion, as well as political corruption. In 2014 a major scandal was uncovered when an organised crime network approached mayor Ignazio Marino; among those investigated (and later sentenced to time in prison) for embezzling public funds was the former mayor Gianni Alemanno. After this impropriety, Italy's Senate passed an anti-corruption bill.

Virginia Raggi of the populist Five Star Movement (M5S) became Rome's first female mayor when she was elected in 2016. In 2021, Raggi was succeeded by centre-left Roberto Gualtieri, who took

Roberto Gualtieri, Mayor of Rome

office with an agenda focusing mainly on public transport, waste management and decorum. He also helmed preparations of the city for the 2025 Catholic Jubilee: new underpasses rerouted traffic from freshly pedestrianised areas, additional metro stations were opened, and monuments restored. In December 2024, in an attempt to halt the rapid proliferation of short-term rentals, Italy banned the use of self-check-in key boxes, claiming the lack of visual identification of guests increased the risk of terrorism. On Christmas Day, Pope Francis opened the holy doors of St Peter's Basilica and kicked off the Catholic Jubilee, which is expected to draw 32 million visitors throughout 2025. Only months later, on 21 April, Pope Francis dies at the age of 88. At the time of writing, preparations were underway for the conclave – the secret meeting where cardinals elect a new pope.

Chronology

753 BC Foundation of Rome.
510 BC Expulsion of Etruscans. Roman Republic established.
31 BC Augustus becomes first Roman emperor.
AD 69–79 Emperor Vespasian has the Colosseum built.
98–117 The Empire achieves its greatest expansion under Trajan.
476 Fall of the Western Roman Empire.

15th century Rome prospers during the Renaissance, attracting such artistic masters as Botticelli, Caravaggio, Michelangelo, Raphael and Titian.

1527 Army of Charles V of Spain sacks Rome.

1585–90 Pope Sixtus V commissions Fontana, Bernini, Borromini and Maderno to build churches, palaces, squares and fountains.

17th century The Italian peninsula fragments into numerous smaller states, among them the Papal States, with Rome as their capital.

1801 Under Napoleon, Rome is made part of the French Empire.

1915 Italy joins Allies in World War I.

1922 Mussolini's march on Rome.

1940 Italy joins Germany in World War II.

1944 Rome liberated. King Vittorio Emanuele III abdicates.

1957 Fledgling European Union established under Treaty of Rome.

2008 Silvio Berlusconi elected prime minister for the third time.

2011 Pope John Paul II beatified. Berlusconi resigns over debt crisis.

2013 Benedict XVI retires and is succeeded by Pope Francis.

2014 Democrat Matteo Renzi forms new government.

2016 Two earthquakes hit Central Italy, killing thousands.

2018 Births drop to the lowest level since 1861. Residents of Rome protest against the collapse of public transport, uncollected rubbish and potholed roads.

2021 Democrat Roberto Gualtieri is elected mayor. He is tasked with renovating monuments and improving the visitor experience in preparation for the 2025 Catholic Jubilee.

2021 Italy wins the postponed UEFA Euro 2020 football tournament; the opening match was held at the Stadio Olimpico in June.

2024 In an attempt to reduce the number of short-term rentals in Rome and other cities, Italy bans the use of self-check-in key boxes.

2025 Pope Francis dies on 21 April at the age of 88, only months after inaugurating the 2025 Jubilee.

The Spanish Steps, one of Rome's main gathering points

Places

Nowhere are the cultural and artistic relics of different eras so seamlessly interwoven as in Rome, from a pagan mausoleum moonlighting as a papal fortress, to a medieval church fronted by a Baroque facade and a Renaissance palace overlooking a modern traffic junction. It doesn't matter whether you've come to Rome for the grandeur of the ancient remains, the revered pilgrimage sites of the Catholic Church or the inspired works of Michelangelo, Raphael and Bernini – you'll end up seeing a glorious hotchpotch of them all. Although the municipality of Rome sprawls over a huge area, the principal sights are packed into a comparatively small zone. For the most part, the best way of exploring the city is on foot. Much of the historic centre has been closed to traffic and parking is generally impossible. Though still lagging behind the efficiency of other European capitals, Rome's public transport has been improved in recent years and will usually deposit you near enough to your destination.

Piazza Venezia and Capitoline Hill

Highlights
- **Vittoriano**, see page 33
- **Capitoline Hill**, see page 34
- **Musei Capitolini**, see page 36

The most convenient place to begin exploring is **Piazza Venezia** ❶. The hub of the capital's main traffic arteries, this is a principal stop on several major bus routes and close to a number of significant sights. As far as orientation is concerned, the **Vittoriano** (Vittorio Emanuele II Monument; https://vive.cultura.gov.it/en/vittoriano; charge) is a landmark visible from all over the city, and provides one of the best views of central Rome. Some Romans wish

> **NOTES**
>
> Many museums are closed on Mondays (the Forum, Colosseum, Palatine and the Vatican Museums are notable exceptions), 1 January and 25 December. In the majority of cases, last entry is one hour before closing.

the dazzling white marble monument were not quite so conspicuous, however, and heap upon it such derisive nicknames as 'Rome's false teeth' and 'The wedding cake'. Built from 1885 to 1911 to celebrate the unification of Italy and dedicated to the new nation's first king, the Vittoriano contains the **Altare della Patria**, the tomb of Italy's Unknown Soldier of World War I. The monument also has a museum complex, with important temporary art exhibitions in its western wing (www.ilvittoriano.com). Once you have climbed to the Altare della Patria, a lift offers access to a panorama of the city.

On the west side of the piazza is **Palazzo Venezia**, the first great Renaissance palace in Rome (www.museopalazzovenezia.beniculturali.it; charge). It was once the embassy of the Venetian Republic to the Holy See, and in the twentieth century served as Mussolini's headquarters. His desk stood at the far corner of the Sala del Mappamondo, positioned to intimidate visitors, who had to approach via some 21 metres (70ft) of marble floor. From the balcony over the central door, *Il Duce* harangued crowds in the square below. The palace shelters a museum of medieval and Renaissance furniture, arms, tapestries, ceramics and sculpture.

Capitoline Hill

Two flights of steps lead up behind the Vittorio Emanuele Monument. The more graceful, **La Cordonata**, takes you between statues of Castor and Pollux (mythical twin sons of Leda and the Swan) to the tranquil elegance of the **Piazza del Campidoglio** on top of the **Capitoline Hill**. This was once the Capitol, where the Temple of Jupiter Optimus Maximus Capitolinus stood, ancient Rome's most sacred site. Today the Campidoglio is a fine Renaissance square, designed by Michelangelo (who also designed La Cordonata) for the reception of the Holy Roman Emperor Charles V. Michelangelo also remodelled the existing **Palazzo Senatorio**, Rome's former town hall, and planned the two palaces that flank it, the Palazzo dei Conservatori and the Palazzo Nuovo, which were completed after his death. Michelangelo had the magnificent second-century AD bronze **statue of Marcus Aurelius** placed in the square. The statue is a copy: the original is the centrepiece of the glass-covered **Sala Marco Aurelio** in the Musei Capitolini. The sculpture survived destruction after the decline

The gleaming white Vittoriano Monument

of Rome because it was mistaken for a likeness of the Christian emperor Constantine, rather than of the pagan Marcus Aurelius.

The **Musei Capitolini** ❷ (www.museicapitolini.org; charge), in the palaces of the Campidoglio, shelters extensive collections of sculpture excavated from ancient Rome. Enter through the courtyard of the **Palazzo dei Conservatori**, where you will encounter a giant marble head, hand and foot, fragments from a 12-metre (40ft) statue of Emperor Constantine II. The palace is also home to the *Capitoline She-Wolf* depicted suckling the infants Romulus and Remus. This Etruscan or medieval bronze has become the symbol of Rome. In the top-floor **Pinacoteca Capitolina** (Capitoline Picture Gallery) are fine works by Caravaggio, Tintoretto, Velázquez, Rubens and Titian.

An underground passageway lined with artefacts connects the Palazzo dei Conservatori with the **Palazzo Nuovo**. The latter

THE FIRST CAPITOL HILL

To the Romans, the Capitol was both citadel and sanctuary, the symbolic centre of government, where the consuls took their oath and the Republic's coinage was minted. Its name originated when a human skull was unearthed during excavations for the Temple of Jupiter and interpreted as a sign that Rome would one day be head *(caput)* of the world.

When the Gauls sacked Rome in 390 BC, the Capitol was saved by the timely cackling of the sanctuary's sacred geese, warning that attackers were scaling the rocks. Later, victorious caesars ended their triumphal processions here. They rode up from the Forum in chariots drawn by white horses to pay homage at the magnificent gilded Temple of Jupiter, which dominated the southern tip of the Capitoline.

In the Middle Ages, the collapsed temples were pillaged, and the hill was abandoned to goats until, in the sixteenth century, Pope Paul III commissioned Michelangelo to give the Campidoglio its new glory.

contains rows of portrait busts of Roman emperors, although its highlights are the poignant statue of the *Dying Gaul*, the sensual *Capitoline Venus*, a Roman copy of a Greek original dating from the second century BC, and the marble *Red Faun*.

Alongside the Palazzo Senatorio a cobbled road opens out onto a terrace, giving you the best view of the Roman Forum ruins (see page 39), stretching from the Arch of Septimius Severus to the Arch of Titus, with the Colosseum beyond. The steeper flight of steps up the Campidoglio climbs to the church of **Santa Maria in Aracoeli** on the site of the temple of Juno Moneta. The thirteenth-century church is the home of the much-revered *Santo Bambino* (Baby Jesus), kept in a separate chapel. The original statue, believed to have miraculous powers, was stolen in 1994 and has been replaced with a copy.

Bronze statue of Constantine, Palazzo dei Conservatori

Ancient Rome

Highlights
- **The Imperial Fora**, see page 38
- **The Roman Forum**, see page 39
- **The Palatine Hill**, see page 44
- **The Colosseum**, see page 45

> **NOTES**
>
> The combination ticket that covers entry into the Colosseum, Palatine Hill and the Roman Forum is valid for 24 hours or two days, depending on which option you choose. Buying it online at www.colosseo.it should save queuing time but online tickets sell faster than the ones at the counter, in which case queueing will be the only option. Another possibility is the seven-day Archeologia Card, which covers even more ancient sites.

The heart of ancient Rome is the area around the Colosseum (see page 45), with the Imperial Fora and Roman Forum to the northwest and the Baths of Caracalla (see page 47) to the south. There's no point in attempting to decipher each fragment of broken stone – not even archaeologists have succeeded in working out what it all was. It's a far better idea to soak up the romantic atmosphere while reflecting on the ruined majesty of this ancient civilisation. Take care to avoid summer's midday sun, as the Forum provides no shade.

The Imperial Fora

Begin at the **Fori Imperiali** (Imperial Fora), which were built as an adjunct to the Foro Romano in honour of Julius Caesar, Augustus, Trajan, Vespasian and Nerva. At the northern end of Trajan's Forum stands the remarkable 30-metre (100ft) **Trajan's Column** (Colonna Traiana; AD 113). Celebrating Trajan's campaigns against the Dacians in what is now Romania, the intricate friezes spiralling around the column constitute a veritable textbook of Roman warfare, featuring embarkation on ships, the clash of armies and the surrender of Barbarian chieftains – in all, using some 2500 figures. St Peter's statue atop the column replaced the Emperor's in 1587.

At **Trajan's Forum** (Foro di Traiano), which can only be viewed from Via dei Fori Imperiali, you can see some of the best-preserved ancient Roman streets and the semi-circular **Trajan's Markets** ❸

(Mercati di Traiano), an ancient shopping mall, made up of 150 shops and offices. The multi-tiered **Trajan's Forum Museum** (www.mercatiditraiano.it; charge) provides an insight into the history and restoration of the site. A **Tourist Information Point** (www.turismoroma.it) on the Via dei Fori Imperiali, between Via Cavour and the Colosseum metro stop, gives useful information about the Imperial Fora and ongoing excavation work there.

The Roman Forum
You can stand among the columns, porticoes and arches of the **Roman Forum** ❹ (Foro Romano; www.colosseo.it; charge) and, with an exhilarating leap of imagination, picture the hub of the

Trajan's Markets

great Imperial City. Surrounded by the Palatine, Capitoline and Esquiline hills, the flat valley of the Forum developed as the civic, commercial and religious centre of the city. Under the emperors, it attained unprecedented splendour, with white marble and golden roofs of temples, law courts and market halls glittering in the sun.

After the Barbarian invasions, the area was abandoned. Subsequent fire, earthquakes, floods and plunder by Renaissance architects reduced the area to a muddy cow pasture, until excavations in the nineteenth century once again brought many of the ancient edifices to light. Grass still grows between the cracked paving stones of the Via Sacra, poppies bloom among the piles of toppled marble and tangles of red roses are entwined in the brick columns, softening the harshness of the ruins.

Audio-guides can be hired at the entrance on Via dei Fori Imperiali at Piazza Santa Maria Nova 53, or you can find your own way around. Before you begin, it's a good idea to orientate yourself with a detailed map, so that you can trace the layout of the ruins and make sense of the apparent confusion.

Ideally, start at the west end, just below the Campidoglio's Palazzo Senatorio (see page 35). Here you can see how the arches of the Roman record office *(Tabularium)* have been incorporated into the rear of the Renaissance palace. Look along the length of the **Via Sacra** (Sacred Way), the route taken by generals as they rode in triumphal procession to the foot of the Capitoline Hill, followed by the legions' standards, ranks of prisoners and carts piled with the spoils of war.

The First Senate House
To counterbalance this image of the Romans as ruthless military conquerors, turn to the brick-built **Curia**, home of the Roman Senate, in the Forum's northwest corner. Here you can gaze through the bronze doors (copies of the originals, which are now in the church of San Giovanni in Laterano; see page 88) at the

'venerable great-grandmother of all parliaments', where the senators, robed in togas, argued the affairs of Republic and Empire. The tenets of Roman law, which underpin most European legal systems, were first debated here. Diocletian constructed the present building in AD 303, and its plain brick facade was once adorned with marble. The church that covered it was dismantled in 1937 to reveal an ancient floor set with geometrical patterns in red and green marble, as well as tiers on either side where the senators sat, and the brick base of the golden statue of Victory at the rear. The Curia shelters two bas-reliefs, outlining in marble the buildings of the Forum.

In front of the Curia, a concrete shelter protects the underground site of the **Lapis Niger** (usually not on view), a black marble stone

The Temple of Saturn

The Temple of Castor and Pollux

placed by Silla over the (presumed) grave of Romulus, the city's founder. Beside it is a stele (a stone slab) engraved with one of the oldest Latin inscriptions ever found, dating back to the sixth century BC; it has not yet been deciphered but it is thought to be a 'no trespassing' sign.

The triple **Arco di Settimio Severo** (Arch of Septimius Severus) dominates this end of the Forum. Its friezes depict the eastern military triumphs of the third-century emperor who later campaigned as far as Scotland. Nearby is the orators' platform, or **Rostra**. Its name comes from the iron prows *(rostra)* that once adorned it, taken from enemy ships at the Battle of Antium in 338 BC. Two points in the Rostra have particular significance: the *Umbilicus Urbis Romae* marks the traditional epicentre of Rome, and the *Miliarium Aureum* (Golden Milestone) recorded in gold letters the distances in miles from Rome to the cities of the far-flung Empire.

Public meetings and ceremonies took place in front of the Rostra, kept bare save for samples of three plants considered sacred to Mediterranean prosperity: the vine, the olive and the fig. Still prominent above this open space is the **Colonna di Foca** (Column of Phocas), built to honour the Byzantine emperor who presented the Pantheon to Pope Boniface IV.

Eight tall columns standing on a podium at the foot of the Capitol belong to the **Tempio di Saturno** (Temple of Saturn), one of the earliest temples in Rome. It doubled as both state treasury and centre of the December debauchery known as the Saturnalia, the pagan precursor of Christmas.

Of the **Basilica Giulia**, which was once busy law courts named after Julius Caesar who commissioned it, only the paving and some of the arches and travertine pillars survive. Even less remains of the Basilica Aemilia, on the opposite side of the Via Sacra, destroyed by the Goths in AD 410.

Three columns, the podium and part of the entablature denote the **Tempio dei Castori** (Temple of Castor and Pollux), built in 484 BC. It was dedicated to the twin sons of Leda and the Swan, after they appeared at Lake Regillus to rally the Romans against the Latins and Etruscans.

Caesar's End

The altar of Julius Caesar is tucked away in a semicircular recess of the **Tempio di Giulio Cesare** (Temple of Julius Caesar). On 19 March in 44 BC, the grieving crowds, following Caesar's funeral procession to his cremation in the Campus Martius, made an impromptu pyre of chairs and tables and burned his body in the Forum instead.

Pause for a pleasant idyll in the **Casa delle Vestali** (House of the Vestal Virgins), surrounded by graceful statues in the serene setting of a rose garden and old rectangular fountain basins, once more filled with water. In the circular white marble **Tempio di Vesta** (Temple of Vesta), the sacred flame perpetuating the Roman state was tended by six Vestal Virgins who, from childhood, observed a thirty-year vow of chastity under threat of being buried alive if they broke it. They were supervised by the high priest, the Pontifex Maximus (the popes have since appropriated this title), of which only brick vestiges remain.

The imposing **Tempio di Antonino e Faustina** (Temple of Antoninus and Faustina), further along the Via Sacra, has survived because, like the Curia, it was converted into a church, acquiring a Baroque facade in 1602. Few ancient buildings can match the massive proportions of the **Basilica di Massenzio** (Basilica of Maxentius), started by Maxentius and completed by Constantine. Three giant vaults still stand.

The Via Sacra culminates in the **Arco di Tito** (Arch of Titus), built to commemorate the capture of Jerusalem in AD 70. Restored by Giuseppe Valadier in 1821, it shows in magnificent carved relief the triumphal procession of Titus bearing the spoils of the city, among them the Temple of Jerusalem's altar, a seven-branched golden menorah and silver trumpets.

The Palatine Hill

From this end of the Forum a slope leads up to the **Palatine Hill** ❺ (Palatino; www.colosseo.it; charge). Rome's legendary birthplace, today it's the city's most romantic garden, dotted with toppled columns among the wildflowers and spiny acanthus shrubs. At the time of the ancient Republic, this was a desirable residential district for the wealthy and aristocratic, including Cicero and Crassus. Augustus began the Imperial trend and later emperors added and expanded, each trying to outdo the last until the whole area was one immense palace (hence the name of the hill). From the pavilions and terraces of the sixteenth-century gardens laid out here by the Farnese family, there is a superb view of the whole Forum. A small **museum** (follow the signs) displays artefacts found nearby.

Just west of the gardens is the **Casa di Augusto** (House of Augustus), where Augustus lived in around 30 BC before he gained supreme power and built his imperial palace complex just along the hill. The rooms, splashed with exquisite frescoes in red, blue and ochre, were opened after years of painstaking restoration. The **Casa di Livia** (House of Livia), which was occupied by his ambitious and scheming wife, also has fine frescoes and wall mosaics. Both houses can be visited only by guided tour (booking required; www.colosseo.it). Nearby, three circular Iron-Age dwellings unearthed from the time of Rome's legendary beginnings are known as the **Capanne di Romolo** (Romulus' Huts).

A passageway, the **Criptoportico**, linked the Palatine buildings to Nero's palace, the **Domus Aurea**. In the dim light you can just make out stucco decorations on the ceilings and walls at one end.

The vast assemblage of ruins of the **Domus Flavia** includes a basilica, throne room, banqueting hall, baths, porticoes and a fountain in the form of a maze. Together with the **Domus Augustana**, the complex is known as the **Palace of Domitian**. You can peer down into the Stadium of Domitian, which was probably a venue for horse races.

Inside the Colosseum

The last emperor to build on the Palatine, Septimius Severus, carried the imperial palace right to the hill's southeastern end, so that his **Domus Severiana** was the impressive first glimpse of the capital for new arrivals. It was dismantled and its expanses of marble were used to build Renaissance Rome.

From this edge of the hill you have a great view down into the immense grassy stretch of the **Circus Maximus** ❻, where vast crowds watched chariot races from tiers of marble seats.

The Colosseum

More than any church or palace, it is the **Colosseum** ❼ that is the symbol of the city's eternity (Colosseo; www.colosseo.it; charge).

Built between AD 72 and AD 80, the four-tiered amphitheatre seated some 50,000 spectators on stone benches, according to social status.

The gladiators were originally criminals, war captives and slaves: later, free men entered the 'profession', tempted by wealth and fame. Contrary to popular belief, there is little historical evidence to support the image of the Colosseum as the place where Christians were fed to the lions. The first stage of the restoration was completed in 2016, which saw the reopening of the underground, hypogeum and the third ring, boasting incredible views of the city (www.colosseo.it; guided tours only).

The top two levels opened for guided visits a year later. Popes and princes stripped the Colosseum of its marble cladding, and its travertine and metal for their churches and palaces. They left behind a ruined maze of cells and corridors that funnelled men and beasts to the slaughter. The horror has been somewhat diluted over the centuries, but the thrill of the monument's titanic endurance remains. As an Anglo-Saxon prophecy says: "While stands the Colosseum, Rome shall stand; when falls the Colosseum, Rome shall fall; and when Rome falls, with it shall fall the world."

The nearby **Arco di Costantino** (Arch of Constantine) celebrates Constantine's victory over

The Arch of Constantine

his imperial rival Maxentius at Saxa Rubra. He may have won the battle, but a cost-conscious Senate decorated the arch with pieces from monuments of earlier rulers Trajan, Hadrian and Marcus Aurelius. Immediately northeast of the Colosseum is the **Domus Aurea** (www.colosseo.it; open Fri–Sun only), once a glorious 250-room villa with extensive gardens built by the emperor Nero, who spent very few years in his 'Golden House' before killing himself in AD 68. Very little remains of the lavish mosaics, frescoes, inlaid floors and paintings in gold.

Baths of Caracalla

The huge third-century AD **Terme di Caracalla** ❽, 1km (0.6 miles) south of the Colosseum, were built for people to bathe in luxury (www.museiitaliani.it; charge). Public bathing was a social event. Senators and merchants passed from the *caldarium* (hot room) to cool down in the *tepidarium* and the *frigidarium*. The baths ran dry in the sixth century when Barbarians cut the aqueducts, but many stunning mosaics remain. Now, in the summer, the baths become the setting for spectacular open-air operas. Previously, the ruins themselves were used as a stage, but nowadays in order to help preserve what is left of the baths, a separate structure has been built in the grounds and the ruins serve as a majestic backdrop.

Centro Storico

Highlights
- **The Pantheon**, see page 48
- **Piazza Navona**, see page 50
- **Sant'Ignazio**, see page 52
- **Palazzo Doria Pamphili**, see page 52
- **Il Gesù**, see page 53
- **Crypta Balbi**, see page 54

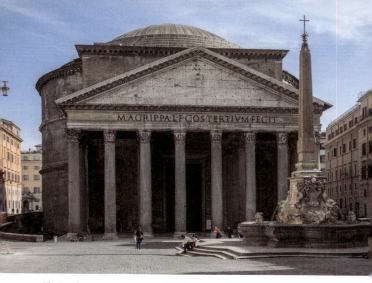

The Pantheon, 'Temple of all the Gods'

The heart of Rome's historic centre is the area tucked within a bend of the River Tiber. Here, on what was once the exercise ground of Roman soldiers known as the Campus Martius or 'Field of Mars', you will find vestiges of Rome's many different eras. Next to the remains of ancient temples there is a maze of medieval streets, as well as graceful Renaissance *palazzi*, ornate Baroque churches, sublime piazzas and spectacular fountains. But the city centre is not entirely a monument to the past – alongside the stunning historical relics, you'll find contemporary shops, hotels and businesses.

The Pantheon

The magnificent **Pantheon** ❾ (www.pantheonroma.com; charge) in the Piazza della Rotonda is ancient Rome's best-preserved monument. This 'Temple of All the Gods' and its elegant hemispherical dome was saved for posterity when it was converted into a church in the seventh century. The original Pantheon, built in 27 BC by Marcus Agrippa (son-in-law of Augustus), burned down. Emperor Hadrian rebuilt it around AD 125, but modestly left his predecessor's name on the frieze above the portico, supported by sixteen monolithic pink-and-grey granite columns. The bronze beams that once adorned the entrance were removed by the Barberini Pope Urban VIII to make Bernini's *baldacchino* canopy for the high altar in St Peter's. His action prompted the saying: "*Quod non fecerunt barbari, fecerunt Barberini*" ("What the Barbarians didn't do, the Barberini did").

The Pantheon's true greatness is only fully appreciated once you step inside and look up into the magnificent coffered **dome**. Over 43 metres (141ft) in diameter (exactly equal to its height), it is even wider than the cupola of St Peter's Basilica. Held up without

WHERE TO SHOOT THE BEST PICTURES

Piazza Navona is Rome's most-photographed square. Arrive in the late afternoon for the best light and lively crowd action. The elegant buildings and fountains are a great contrast to the bars dotting the piazza, so try to include both in one shot to capture the feel. For a great photo of the Colosseum, you'll need to gain some distance from it, for example, from the top of Colle Oppio; best at sunset or dawn. Early morning is a good time to photograph the Trevi Fountain, as the light is excellent, and the hordes haven't descended yet. The statues are a great background for a portrait picture. At sunset, light reflects beautifully from the Tiber onto Castel Sant'Angelo; set up your shot from across the river to include the bridge and the angel statue. There isn't a bad time to photograph the Pantheon and its piazza, though they are at their most wonderful at night after the sun has set. Inside, shoot looking up at the domed roof, where natural light floods through the oculus. To snap decent photos of the Roman Forum, arrive early and hotfoot it to the top of the Palatine for a fine vantage point. In spring the wisterias are in bloom, adding a beautiful splash of colour.

> ### BERNINI AND THE BAROQUE
>
> Although more restrained than elsewhere in Europe, Roman Baroque is theatrical, bold and at times bombastic. At the forefront was architect and sculptor, Gian Lorenzo Bernini (1598–1680), whose style found favour with a succession of popes. Even St Peter's is, in part, a Bernini creation, graced by enfolding, keyhole-shaped colonnades. Other masterpieces include the witty design for an elephant to bear the obelisk of Santa Maria sopra Minerva and the angels on Ponte Sant'Angelo. Palazzo Barberini (1629–33) heralded the Baroque style and was completed by Bernini, assisted by Borromini, who became his arch-rival.

any sustaining columns or flying buttresses, it is an unparalleled feat of engineering. On fine days a shaft of sunlight illuminates the windowless vault through the circular hole *(oculus)* in the dome, and it is through this opening that thousands of rose petals are dropped each year in a striking ceremony to mark Pentecost. The gods and goddesses that were once inside the Pantheon are long gone, replaced by the Renaissance tombs of Raphael (and his mistress) and the architect Baldassarre Peruzzi, as well as the first king of Italy.

Piazza Navona

A short walk west of the Pantheon is the beautiful **Piazza Navona** ❿, the heart of the northern half of the Centro Storico and a prime spot for recreation since the time of Emperor Domitian, who laid out an athletics arena, Circus Agonalis, on this site in AD 79, establishing the future piazza's oval shape.

Jousting tournaments took place here in the Middle Ages, and from the seventeenth to the nineteenth century it was the scene of spectacular water pageants in summer, when the fountains overflowed until the piazza was flooded. Today the square remains Rome's perfect stage set, and the public spectacle continues.

Secure a front-row seat at any of the alfresco cafés and enjoy the show supplied by artists, performers, musicians and caricaturists.

The Baroque centrepiece of the piazza is Bernini's **Fontana dei Quattro Fiumi** (Fountain of the Four Rivers), which incorporates an ancient obelisk into a monumental allegory symbolising the great rivers of the four continents: the Americas (Río de la Plata), Europe (the Danube), Asia (the Ganges) and Africa (the Nile). Romans who delight in Bernini's scorn for his rivals suggest that the Nile god is covering his head rather than having to look at Borromini's church of Sant'Agnese in Agone, and that the river god of the Americas is poised to catch it in case it collapses. In fact, the fountain was completed some years before Borromini's fine facade and dome – but it is an entertaining rumour, nonetheless.

A brief walk north from the piazza leads to the **Palazzo Altemps** ⓫, a branch of the Museo Nazionale Romano (www.museonazionaleromano.beniculturali.it; charge; see page 86), which features the magnificent **Boncompagni Ludovisi collection** in a gorgeous sixteenth-century palace containing frescoed halls, a painted loggia, a church, a theatre and a beautiful internal courtyard. Among the most important pieces is

Fountain of the Four Rivers in Piazza Navona

> **NOTES**
>
> The pedestrian-only Via dei Pastini leads east from the Piazza della Rotonda and forms the beginning of a tourist drag that takes in the columns of the Tempio di Adriano, as well as ice-cream outlets and souvenir shops, before crossing the Via del Corso and eventually reaching the Trevi Fountain (see page 62).

the marble altar top known as the *Ludovisi Throne*, thought to be an original Greek work from the fifth century BC, with exquisitely carved reliefs of Aphrodite and a maiden playing the flute. Also, seek out the tragic *Suicide of a Galatian*, the statue of a Barbarian warrior in the act of killing himself and his wife rather than submit to slavery. Other highlights include the colossal head of Juno and the equally gigantic sarcophagus featuring intricate scenes of battle between Romans and Barbarians. Victory over the Barbarians was a much-favoured decorative theme between the second half of the second century AD and the first half of the third century AD.

East of the Pantheon

In an enchanting setting of russet and ochre rococo housing is the seventeenth-century church of **Sant'Ignazio** (http://santignazio.gesuiti.it; free). Inside, Fra Andrea Pozzo (himself a Jesuit priest) painted a *trompe l'oeil* **ceiling fresco** (1685) depicting St Ignatius' entry into paradise. Stand on a buff stone disc in the nave's central aisle and gaze up; you will have the impression of the building rising up and away far above you. Viewed from any other point inside the church, the columns appear to collapse. From another disc further up the aisle, you can admire the celestial dome above the Baroque altar.

South of here, around the corner from the Piazza del Collegio Romano, is the vast **Palazzo Doria Pamphili** ⓬ (also spelt Pamphilj; Via del Corso 305; www.doriapamphilj.it), the private residence of the important Doria family. The family's rich collection of paintings was assembled over hundreds of years. There are a number of masterpieces from the fifteenth to the seventeenth century, including works by Raphael, Titian, Tintoretto, Veronese and Caravaggio, as well as paintings from the Dutch and Flemish schools. Look out for the evocative landscape of the *Flight into Egypt* by Annibale Carracci, Caravaggio's *Penitent Magdalene* and the windswept *Naval Battle in the Bay of Naples* by Brueghel the Elder. You'll find a nice stylistic contrast in a little room off to the side of the galleries; Velázquez's brilliant worldly portrait of *Innocent X*, the Pamphili family pope, alongside a more serene marble bust of him by Bernini.

South of the Pantheon

Streets on either side of the Pantheon lead south to the Largo di Torre Argentina and across the main road to the **Area Sacra Argentina**, the excavated remains of four temples dating from the third to first century BC (viewed from the road only).

On the other side of Largo Argentina is **Il Gesù** ⓭, the mother church of the Jesuits and a major element in their Counter-Reformation campaign. Begun as their Roman headquarters in 1568, its open plan became the model for the congregational churches that were intended

Area Sacra Argentina

to wrest popular support from the Protestants. While its facade is more sober than the subsequent Baroque churches, the interior glorifies the new militancy in bronze, gold, marble and precious stones.

St Ignatius Loyola, a Spanish soldier who founded the order, has a fittingly magnificent tomb under an altar in the left transept, with a profusion of lapis lazuli, a thin shell fused to plaster stucco.

Just to the south, on the Via delle Botteghe Oscure, is the **Crypta Balbi** (https://museonazionaleromano.beniculturali.it; currently closed for restoration), part of the Museo Nazionale Romano. Set on the site of the portico of the Imperial Roman Theatre of Balbus, the museum documents the changing faces of Rome through history.

Around the Campo de' Fiori

The hub of the southern section of the Centro Storico is the **Campo de' Fiori** ⓴, once the site of public executions during the seventeenth century, now a lively fruit, vegetable and flower market, one of Rome's most attractive and authentic. A reminder of the square's bloody history, however, is provided by the brooding statue of philosopher Giordano Bruno, who was burned alive during the Counter-Reformation in 1600.

Just south of the Campo is another lovely square, Piazza Farnese. Here, the great architects of the age worked on the **Palazzo Farnese** ⓯, Rome's finest Renaissance palace. Begun in 1514 by Antonio da Sangallo the Younger for Cardinal Farnese (Pope Paul III), the project was passed on to Michelangelo, who was responsible for the top floor, and was completed in 1589 by Giacomo della Porta. The building cost so much that it put a great strain on the fortune Farnese had amassed while he was treasurer of the Church. The palace is now the French Embassy, and you need to book a guided tour to see the dining room's mythological frescoes by Annibale Carracci (www.visite-palazzofarnese.it; charge). Facing Palazzo Farnese, to the left of the square, is **Palazzo Spada** (www.gebart.it; charge), a beautiful example of Renaissance art, which houses

Market stalls at Campo de' Fiori

the art collection of Cardinal Spada in its original setting, including the *trompe l'oeil* trickery of Borromini's famed Perspective Gallery.

Nearby, housed in an elegant Renaissance mansion, is the **Museo Barracco** (Corso Vittorio Emanuele 166/A; www.museobarracco.it; free). The museum is devoted to ancient sculpture, not just from Rome but from Assyria, Egypt, Cyprus, Phoenicia, Etruria and Greece as well. Highlights of this wonderful collection include works by the Greek sculptor Polyclitus, engraved marble slabs recovered in the Mesopotamian cities of Nineveh and Nimrud, and a head of Heracles from Cyprus.

The Jewish Ghetto

Retrace your steps to the Campo de' Fiori. The narrow streets heading southeast of the marketplace take you into the former **Jewish**

Ghetto, a lively and historic district peppered with restaurants serving the city's distinctive Roman–Jewish cuisine. Pope Paul IV forced Jews into this confined space in 1555. Rules were relaxed considerably after his death, but the walls that confined the quarter were not torn down until 1848. A small but vibrant Jewish community still lives in and around the Via del Portico d'Ottavia. The main synagogue sits by the riverbank. One of the most delightful fountains in Rome, and much loved by children, is the sixteenth-century **Fontana delle Tartarughe** (Turtle Fountain), in Piazza Mattei. It depicts four boys perched on dolphins while lifting four turtles onto an upper marble basin, with gracefully outstretched arms.

Fontana della Barcaccia and the Spanish Steps

Nearby is the **Portico d'Ottavia**, a crumbling and arched facade more than 2000 years old and dedicated to Augustus' sister. Beyond it extends the **Teatro di Marcello** ⓰ (Theatre of Marcellus), begun by Julius Caesar, finished under Augustus and said to be the architectural model for the Colosseum.

A short way to the southeast is the little church of **Santa Maria in Cosmedin**, which was given by the Pope to Rome's Greek colony in the eighth century. Its Romanesque facade and simple interior, with beautiful floor mosaics, provide a stark contrast to the city's dominant Baroque grandeur. Test your honesty in the portico's fierce-looking **Bocca della Verità** (Mouth of Truth), made famous by Audrey Hepburn in the 1953 film *Roman Holiday*, on the left wall of the portico. Think twice about putting your hand inside the mouth of the twelfth-century marble face; it is said to bite off the fingers of liars.

Across the road, two of the city's best-preserved temples stand on what was part of the ancient cattle market. The **Tempio Rotondo** ⓱, with its twenty fluted Corinthian columns, was probably dedicated to Hercules and is the oldest standing marble temple in Rome. Its rectangular neighbour, the **Tempio di Fortuna Virile**, is a victim of an ancient typing error, as its presiding deity is believed to have been Portunus, god of harbours, rather than Fortuna (Fortune). A short walk back on the Lungotevere is the imposing **Great Synagogue** (Lungotevere dei Cenci; www.museoebraico.roma.it; charge) built in 1904, housing a museum that traces the history of the Roman Jewish Community.

Spanish Steps and Tridente

Highlights
- **Via del Corso**, see page 59
- **Piazza del Popolo**, see page 60
- **Pincio Gardens**, see page 61
- **Augustus' Altar of Peace**, see page 61

The city's most sophisticated shopping district, the area around the **Piazza di Spagna** has been attracting foreigners for centuries. Aristocratic travellers on the Grand Tour came here, as did many of the most celebrated artists of the Romantic era, among them Keats, Byron, Balzac, Wagner and Liszt.

The area continues to attract a cosmopolitan crowd. Well-heeled visitors come for the high-fashion boutiques along Via dei Condotti and its grid of neighbouring cobbled streets. The more casually dressed linger on the glorious and recently restored **Scalinata della Trinità dei Monti** ⓲ – the Spanish Steps, named after the nearby residence of the Spanish Ambassador to the Vatican, a popular meeting place for young Romans and foreigners alike. The steps ascend in three majestic tiers to the sixteenth-century French church of **Trinità dei Monti**. Its twin belfries and graceful Baroque facade make it one of Rome's most distinctive landmarks. The steps are adorned with pink azaleas in spring, and in summer they make a spectacular location for occasional designer fashion shows. Sitting on the steps is banned, and you're likely to be warned off with a sharp whistle from a guard if you plonk yourself down; litter the steps and you may be slapped with a fine of up to €400.

At the foot of the Spanish Steps lies the **Fontana della Barcaccia**, in the shape of a sinking boat. The design, attributed to Pietro Bernini or his far more famous son, Gian Lorenzo Bernini, is an ingenious solution to the problem of low pressure in the Acqua Vergine aqueduct at this point, which supplies the fountain (as well as the nearby Trevi Fountain) with water.

The poet John Keats died of consumption in 1821 at the age of 25 in a small room overlooking the Steps. His house, 26 Piazza di Spagna, has since been preserved as the **Keats-Shelley Museum** (www.keats-shelley-house.org; charge). On the other side of the Steps, at No. 23, **Babingtons** tearooms (www.babingtons.com) is a pleasant old-world bastion of Anglo-Saxon calm and gentility that has been serving tea and scones since the 1890s.

An even more venerable establishment is nearby on Via dei Condotti. **Caffè Greco** (www.anticocaffegreco.eu) has been a favourite haunt of writers and artists ever since it opened in 1760. The autographed portraits, busts and statues attest to its distinguished patrons, among them Casanova, Goethe, Baudelaire, Buffalo Bill, Gogol and Hans Christian Andersen. The thick hot chocolate served here in the winter by frock-coated waiters is a long-standing tradition among stylish Roman shoppers and strollers.

Via del Corso

The **Tridente** area takes its name from the trio of streets built in the sixteenth century to relieve congestion in Rome's cramped medieval centre. Via del Corso, Via di Ripetta and Via del Babuino emanate like the prongs of a fork from the Piazza del Popolo, for centuries the main entrance to Rome for travellers arriving from the north.

The **Via del Corso** is the 1.6km (1 mile) -long main street of central Rome, which runs in a straight line from Piazza Venezia to Piazza del Popolo. Known in ancient times as the Via Lata, the Corso derives its modern name from the carnival races, or *corse*, that were held here in the fifteenth century under the spectacle-loving Venetian Pope Paul II. Of all the races, the most thrilling was the Corsa dei Barberi, in which riderless Barbary horses, sent into a frenzy by saddles spiked with nails, charged pell-mell along the narrow thoroughfare to be halted at last by a large white sheet hung across the street. Today the partly pedestrianised Corso is lined with palaces and churches and crowded with mainly mid-market large shops, department stores and shoppers. The streets shooting off it are full of exclusive boutiques, wineries and cafés.

Caffè Greco

Roughly halfway along the road is the **Piazza Colonna**, where the **column of Marcus Aurelius**, decorated with spiralling reliefs of the Emperor's military triumphs, rises in front of the Italian prime minister's offices in the **Chigi Palace**. The statue of the soldier-emperor that stood on top of the column was replaced in 1589 by one of St Paul.

On the **Piazza di Montecitorio** nearby, dominated by a sixth-century BC Egyptian obelisk, is the **Palazzo Montecitorio**, designed by Bernini for the Ludovisi family. It houses the Camera dei Deputati (Chamber of Deputies), Italy's legislative lower house.

Piazza del Popolo

At its northern, pedestrianised end, the Corso culminates in the graceful oval shape of the **Piazza del Popolo** ⓭, a truly exemplary piece of open-air urban theatre, designed in 1818 by Giuseppe Valadier, former architect to Napoleon. The central obelisk, 24-metres (79ft) high, is from the thirteenth-century BC Egypt of Ramses II. It was brought to Rome by Augustus and erected in the Circus Maximus. Pope Sixtus V had it moved here in 1589.

The square takes its name from the Renaissance church of **Santa Maria del Popolo**, built at the northern gateway to the piazza on the site of Nero's tomb to exorcise his ghost, reputed to haunt the area. In its Baroque interior is a superb fresco of the *Nativity* by the Umbrian painter Pinturicchio in the first chapel on the right, and Raphael's Chigi Chapel, built as a mausoleum for the family of the wealthy Sienese banker and brilliant arts patron, Agostino Chigi. This chapel houses two fine sculptures by Bernini; *Habakkuk* and *Daniel and the Lion*. In the Cerasi Chapel to the left of the altar are two powerful works by Caravaggio, the *Conversion of Saul* and *Crucifixion of St Peter*, notable for the dramatic use of light and shade and the skillful foreshortening of the figures.

The piazza's arched sixteenth-century **Porta del Popolo** marks the gateway to ancient Rome at the end of the Via Flaminia, which led from Rimini on the Adriatic coast. Pilgrims arriving in Rome by this gate were later greeted by the imposing Baroque churches of Santa Maria dei Miracoli and Santa Maria di Montesanto on the southern side, guarding the entrance to the Corso. Two of the most historic and exclusive cafés in Rome, Rosati and Canova, square up to one another across the expanse.

Pincio Gardens

To the east of the piazza and above the Piazza del Popolo and a monumental complex of terraces, the nineteenth-century **Pincio Gardens** offer a panoramic view of the piazza and the city, especially at sunset, when the rooftops are tinged purple and gold. Also the work of Valadier, the statue-peppered gardens occupy the site of the first-century BC villa of Lucius Licinius Lucullus, a provincial governor who returned enriched by the spoils of Asia and impressed his contemporaries with his extravagant lifestyle. The gardens stretch on to the **Villa Borghese park** (see page 66).

Villa Borghese

Lined with pine trees and open-air cafés, the Pincio promenade marches past **Villa Medici**, built in 1564 and bought by Napoleon in 1803 to house the French Academy in Rome. Today the villa remains home to young French artists visiting the city on scholarships and hosts memorable exhibitions and concerts (www.villamedici.it).

Augustus' Altar of Peace

West of the Via del Corso, towards the banks of the River Tiber, is the **Ara Pacis Augustae** (www.arapacis.it; charge) in Piazza Augusto Imperatore, a fascinating monument, which has been renovated and converted into a small museum complex, designed by renowned US architect Richard Meier. After fragments of this 'Altar of Peace', built to celebrate Augustus' victorious campaigns in Gaul and Spain, first came to light in 1568, they were dispersed among several European museums. Most of the pieces were returned to Rome when the building's reconstruction began in the 1930s. The friezes depict Augustus with his wife Livia and daughter Julia, his friend Agrippa and a host of priests and dignitaries. Alongside the altar, the great mound encircled by cypresses is the **Mausoleo di Augusto** (www.mausoleodiaugusto.it; charge; currently closed for restoration), repository of the ashes of the caesars (except Trajan) until Hadrian built his own mausoleum (now the Castel Sant'Angelo, see page 71).

The Trevi Fountain and Quirinale

Highlights
- **Trevi Fountain**, see page 62
- **Palazzo del Quirinale**, see page 63

No matter how many times you see it, the **Fontana di Trevi** ⓴ (Trevi Fountain) never fails to astonish. Nicola Salvi's Baroque extravaganza seems to be a giant stage set, out of all proportion to its tiny piazza. The eighteenth-century fountain is, in fact, a triumphal arch and palace facade (for the old Palazzo Poli), which frames mythical creatures in a riot of rocks, fountains and pools, all theatrically illuminated at night. The

> **NOTES**
>
> Legend has it that throwing using your right hand to throw a coin over your left shoulder into the Trevi Fountain will secure you a return visit to Rome. Donations are made to Caritas, a Catholic charity working to end poverty, from the collected coins.

centrepiece is the massive figure of Oceanus riding on a seashell drawn by a pair of winged sea horses led by tritons. The rearing horse symbolises the sea's turmoil, the calm steed its tranquillity. Anita Ekberg and Marcello Mastroianni frolicked memorably in the fountain's waters (carried by an ancient Roman aqueduct) when they starred in Federico Fellini's 1960 film, *La Dolce Vita* ('The Sweet Life'). After an extensive 2015 restoration that cost upwards of €2m, paid for by luxury fashion brand Fendi, the monument has been returned to its gleaming former glory.

The splendid Baroque Trevi Fountain

Quirinale

Between Piazza Barberini and the Imperial Forum, and dominating the summit of the highest of the seven hills of ancient Rome, is the Baroque **Palazzo del Quirinale** ㉑ (https://palazzo.quirinale. it/visitapalazzo/prenota_en.html; booking required). This was the summer palace of the popes until 1870, when it became home to the new King of Italy. Since 1947, it has been the official residence of the president of the Republic. In the centre of the vast Piazza del Quirinale, magnificent statues of Castor and Pollux and their steeds – all Roman copies of Greek originals – stand beside an ancient obelisk. Also here is the Scuderie del Quirinale (www. scuderiequirinale.it; charge), a large space for major exhibitions.

> **ROME'S PRINCIPAL ARTISTS AND ARCHITECTS**
>
> **Bernini** (1598–1680). The foremost exponent of Baroque, whose works include St Peter's Square, Fountain of the Four Rivers in Piazza Navona, Palazzo Barberini and Galleria Borghese.
> **Borromini** (1599–1667). Baroque architect who designed Sant'Agnese in Agone, Sant'Ivo alla Sapienza and the Palazzo Barberini.
> **Bramante** (1444–1514). The most important architect of the High Renaissance created the Belvedere Courtyard in the Vatican Museums and the tempietto inside San Pietro in Montorio.
> **Michelangelo** (1475–1564). Sculptor, architect, painter, whose creations include the dome of St Peter's Basilica, the Sistine Chapel ceiling, *Moses* in the Church of St Peter in Chains, and the Campidoglio.
> **Caravaggio** (1571–1610). Known for his bold use of foreshortening, dramatic chiaroscuro and earthy realism, Caravaggio's paintings are in Santa Maria del Popolo, San Luigi dei Francesi, Palazzo Barberini, Sant'Agostino, and Galleria Borghese.
> **Pinturicchio** (c.1454–1513). Painter of frescoes in the Sistine Chapel, the Borgia Apartments and Santa Maria del Popolo.
> **Raphael (Raffaello Sanzio)** (1483–1520). Painter and architect of the High Renaissance. Works include the *Stanze di Raffaello* in the Vatican, Chigi Chapel in Santa Maria del Popolo, and *La Fornarina* in Palazzo Barberini.

The piazza affords a splendid view over the whole city towards St Peter's.

Admirers of the Baroque era will find much to delight them in this part of the city, which teems with masterpieces of sculpture and architecture by Bernini. Opposite the *manica lunga* or 'long sleeve' of the Quirinal Palace you will find the small church of **Sant'Andrea al Quirinale**, demonstrating the genius of the seventeenth-century master in its elliptical plan, gilded dome and stucco work. Further along is the tiny **San Carlo alle Quattro Fontane**, by Bernini's arch-rival, Borromini. It may be small, but with its concave and convex surfaces, it is one of Rome's most original church designs.

In the nearby **Piazza Barberini** (at the corner of the Via Veneto) are two of Bernini's celebrated fountains: the **Fontana del Tritone**, which takes centre stage, and the **Fontana delle Api**, on its north side (dedicated to the public and their animals). Both monuments sport the bee symbol taken from the Barberini coat of arms of Pope Urban VIII, Bernini's patron.

The busy genius also had a hand in the architecture of the stately **Palazzo Barberini** ㉒ (1625–33), which now houses part of the **Galleria Nazionale d'Arte Antica** (www.barberinicorsini.org; charge). Situated on the Via delle Quattro Fontane, the building provided another architectural battleground for Bernini and rival Borromini, each of whom built one of its grand staircases and contributed to the facade. It is worth a visit as much for its Baroque decor as for its collection of thirteenth- to seventeenth-century paintings. Don't forget to look up in the Salone or **Great Hall** to see Pietro da Cortona's illusionist ceiling fresco, *Triumph of Divine Providence* (1633–9).

Most of the collection is hung in the first-floor gallery (the rest is in the Palazzo Corsini across the Tiber).

Borromini's San Carlo alle Quattro Fontane

> **VIA VENETO**
>
> Once the site of a palace surrounded by vast gardens and grounds belonging to the Ludovisi family villa, Via Veneto became renowned in the roaring 1950s and 1960s as the focal point of the so-called *Dolce Vita*, or Hollywood-on-the-Tiber. This twisting avenue lined with elegant and fashionable cafés became the hangout for the rich and famous (Audrey Hepburn, James Stewart, Ingrid Bergman and Marcello Mastroianni, to name just a few) who were working at Rome's Cinecittà film studios. Though some of the cafés remain, most of the late nineteenth-century *palazzi* now house impersonal luxury hotels, offices and tourist-orientated restaurants.

Works include a Fra Angelico triptych, a portrait of King Henry VIII by Hans Holbein and paintings by Titian, Tintoretto and El Greco. Two standouts are Raphael's *La Fornarina* ('The Baker's Daughter'), said to be a portrait of his mistress and model for many of his madonnas, and Caravaggio's depiction of *Judith Beheading Holofernes*.

From here, Via Barberini leads to Largo Santa Susanna and the church of **Santa Maria della Vittoria**, home to Bernini's *Ecstasy of St Teresa*, a masterpiece of Baroque sculpture. The Piazza Barberini serves as a base for the Via Veneto (see box), which heads north to the Villa Borghese.

Villa Borghese

Highlights
- **Galleria Borghese**, see page 67
- **Museo Carlo Bilotti**, see page 68
- **Villa Giulia**, see page 68

At the top of Via Veneto, across Piazzale Brasile, is the large and leafy **Villa Borghese** park, once the estate of Cardinal Scipione Borghese, nephew of Pope Paul V. The Galleria Borghese is housed in the cardinal's former summer palace; a collection of modern art is in the former Orangery; and Italy's finest Etruscan art in the Villa Giulia.

Galleria Borghese and Museo Carlo Bilotti

The avid art collector Cardinal Scipione Borghese masterminded this handsome Baroque villa on the eastern side of the park as a home for his small but outstanding collection, using his prestige as the nephew of Pope Paul V to acquire coveted masterpieces. **Galleria Borghese** ㉓ (http://galleriaborghese.beniculturali.it; charge; reservation required at www.gebart.it) is one of Italy's best small museums. The principal highlights are a handful of astonishing sculptures by the cardinal's young protégé, Gian Lorenzo Bernini. These include busts of his patron, a vigorous *David* and a graceful *Apollo and Daphne*, in which the 26-year-old sculptor depicts the water nymph turning into a laurel just as the god is about to seize her. The gallery's star attraction is Canova's portrayal of Napoleon's sister *Pauline* as a reclining Venus (1805): Pauline married into the Borghese family. Exceptional paintings include Raphael's *Deposition*; Titian's *Sacred and Profane Love*; a number of Caravaggio's works, including *David with the Head of Goliath* and the *Madonna of the Serpent*;

Temple on Villa Borghese's lake

> **NOTES**
>
> Villa Borghese Park is not only great for a gentle stroll; you can hire bicycles and rollerblades in the grounds, or take a rowing boat out on the picturesque lake.

along with pieces by Botticelli, Cranach, Dürer and Rubens.

The former Orangery of the Villa Borghese has been transformed into the **Museo Carlo Bilotti** (Viale Fiorello La Guardia; www.museocarlobilotti.it; charge), which houses a precious collection of modern art including the work of de Chirico, Severini, Warhol, and Larry Rivers. Meanwhile, the **Galleria Nazionale d'Arte Moderna e Contemporanea** (National Gallery of Modern and Contemporary Art; http://lagallerianazionale.com; charge) covers the 1800s to the present and features the work of artists such as Henry Moore, Jackson Pollock, Paul Cézanne and Wassily Kandinsky. Lovers of modern art should visit two more museums: the **MACRO** (www.museomacro.org; charge) at Via Nizza 138, with its vast collection by contemporary Italian artists, and the **MAXXI** (www.maxxi.art; charge), located further north on Via Guido Reni 4a in a beautiful white Zaha Hadid building, dedicated to the great art and photography of the twenty-first century.

Villa Giulia

This sixteenth-century pleasure palace built for Pope Julius III in the northwest corner of the Villa Borghese park, is now the setting for Italy's finest **Etruscan Museum** ㉔ (Museo Etrusco; www.museoetru.it; charge). Although much about this pre-Roman civilisation is still a mystery, the Etruscans (found in Tuscany, Umbria and in parts of Lazio, north of Rome) left a wealth of detail about their customs and everyday life in the personal possessions they buried with their dead. Room after room is filled with objects excavated from the tombs: bronze statues of warriors; shields, weapons and chariots;

gold and silver jewellery; decorative vases imported from Greece; and a host of everyday cooking utensils, mirrors and combs.

The Vatican

Highlights
- **Castel Sant'Angelo**, see page 71
- **St Peter's Basilica**, see page 73
- **The Vatican Museums**, see page 76

Possibly the best word to describe the Vatican is 'power', which encompasses the immense size, beauty and spirituality of St

Looking down from the basilica over St Peter's Square

Ponte Sant'Angelo and castle

Peter's Basilica as well as the awe inspired by the splendours of the Vatican City and the corruption often implicit within both. At their best, the popes and cardinals prevented military conquest through moral leadership and persuasion; at their worst, they could show the same hunger for power and wealth as any caesar or grand duke.

Constantine, the first Christian emperor, erected the original St Peter's Basilica in AD 324, over an oratory on the presumed site of the tomb of the Apostle, who was martyred (with St Paul) in Rome in AD 67. After Saracens sacked it in 846, Pope Leo IV ordered walls to be built around the church, and the enclosed area was known as the Leonine City, and then Vatican City, after the Etruscan name of its location.

The Vatican only became the main residence of the popes after 1378, when the papacy was returned to Rome from exile in Avignon. It has been a sovereign state, independent of Italy, since the Lateran Pact signed with Mussolini in 1929. The Pope is supreme ruler of this tiny state, which is guarded by an elite corps of Swiss Guards, founded in 1506, who still wear the blue, scarlet and orange uniforms said to have been designed by Michelangelo. The papal domain has its own newspaper, *L'Osservatore Romano*, and a radio station that broadcasts worldwide. It also has shops, banks, a minuscule and rarely used railway station, and an efficient postal service that issues its own Vatican stamps.

Apart from the one square kilometre (0.4 sq miles) comprising St Peter's Square, St Peter's Basilica, and the papal palace and gardens, the Vatican also has jurisdiction over extraterritorial enclaves, including the basilicas of San Giovanni in Laterano, Santa Maria Maggiore and St Paul's, as well as the Pope's summer residence at Castel Gandolfo, to the southeast of the city (www.museivaticani.va).

You don't need a passport to cross the border, though it is marked by a band of white travertine stones running from the ends of the two colonnades at the rim of St Peter's Square. The **Vatican Tourist Information Office** on the south side of St Peter's Square arranges guided tours and issues tickets to Vatican City, including the gardens. A visit to St Peter's combines well with a tour of Castel Sant'Angelo, but it's best to save the Vatican Museums for a separate day: the 7km (4 miles) of galleries can be overwhelming and are best savoured in small doses.

Castel Sant'Angelo

Cross the Tiber by the **Ponte Sant'Angelo**, which incorporates arches of Hadrian's original bridge, the Pons Aelius, built in AD 134. The balustrades are adorned with ten angels carved by Bernini and his studio between 1598 and 1660, each bearing a symbol of the Passion of Christ.

From the bridge you can take in a perfect view of **Castel Sant'Angelo** ㉕ (http://castelsantangelo.beniculturali.it; charge), its mighty brick walls stripped of their travertine cladding and pitted by cannonballs. Conceived by Hadrian as his family mausoleum, it became part of the defensive Aurelian Wall a century later. The castle gained its present name in AD 590 after Pope Gregory the Great had a vision of the Archangel Michael alighting on a turret and sheathing his sword to signal the end of a plague. For centuries this was Rome's mightiest military bastion and a refuge

Michelangelo's dome in St Peter's Basilica

for popes who, in times of trouble, could reach the castle via an elevated passageway, the **Passetto di Borgo** (www.coopculture.it), linking the Vatican to Castel Sant'Angelo. The Passetto was last used for this purpose in 1527, when Clement VII sequestered himself in the fortress during the sack of Rome by Habsburg troops.

A spiral ramp, showing traces of the original black-and-white mosaic paving, leads up to the funerary chamber where the ashes of emperors were kept in urns. You emerge into the **Cortile dell'Angelo** (Courtyard of the Angel), which is stacked neatly with cannonballs and watched over by a marble angel. An arms museum opens off the courtyard.

After the bleakness of the exterior, it comes as a surprise to step into the luxurious surroundings of the old **Papal Apartments**. Lavish frescoes cover the walls and ceilings of rooms hung with masterpieces by Dosso Dossi, Nicolas Poussin and Lorenzo Lotto. Off the Courtyard of Alexander VI is what must be the most exquisite bathroom in history; just wide enough for its marble tub, it is painted with delicate designs over every inch of its walls and along the side of the bath.

A harsh jolt brings you back to reality as you enter the **dungeons**, the scene of torture and executions. You have to bend over double to crawl into the bare, stone cells where prisoners languished – among them sculptor-goldsmith Benvenuto Cellini and philosopher and monk Giordano Bruno.

The **Gallery of Pius IV**, surrounding the entire building, affords a panoramic view, as does the terrace on the summit, with the eighteenth-century bronze statue of *St Michael* by Verschaffelt. Opera lovers will recall this as the setting for the final act of Puccini's *Tosca*, in which the heroine hurls herself to her death from the battlements.

St Peter's Basilica

From Castel Sant'Angelo, a wide, straight avenue – Via della Conciliazione – leads triumphantly (or menacingly, depending on your state of mind) up to St Peter's. A maze of medieval streets, where Raphael had a studio, was destroyed in 1936 by Mussolini's architects to provide an unobstructed view of St Peter's all the way from the banks of the Tiber. A thick wall running parallel to the avenue conceals the papal passageway *(Il Passetto)* that links the Vatican to the Castel Sant'Angelo (see page 72). In 2024, as part of the renovation works in preparation for the 2025 Catholic Jubilee, Rome created the new Piazza Pia. Traffic has been redirected down to a traffic underpass, clearing the way for the uninterrupted pedestrianised walkway that connects the Vatican, Via della Conciliazione, and Castel Sant'Angelo.

ENTERING ETERNITY

The poet Goethe once said that entering St Peter's is "like entering eternity". The world's largest Roman Catholic church certainly has immense dimensions: 212 metres (695ft) long on the outside, 187 metres (613ft) inside, and 132 metres (433ft) to the tip of the dome. Brass markers on the floor of the central aisle show how far other famous cathedrals fail to measure up.

Caravaggio's Descent from the Cross, Pinacoteca Vaticana

In **Piazza San Pietro** (St Peter's Square), another of Bernini's masterpieces, is one of the world's most exciting pieces of architectural orchestration. The sweeping curves of the colonnades reach out to embrace Rome and draw pilgrims into the bosom of the Church. On Easter Sunday as many as 300,000 people cram into the piazza to hear Mass. The square is on or near the site of Nero's Circus, where early Christians were martyred.

It took Bernini eleven years (1656–67) to complete the 284 travertine columns and 88 pilasters, topped by 140 statues of saints. In the centre rises a 25-metre (82ft) red granite **obelisk**, brought here from Egypt by Caligula in AD 37. Stand on one of the two circular paving stones, set between the obelisk and the twin seventeenth-century fountains, to see the quadruple rows of perfectly aligned Doric columns appear magically as one.

A grandiose achievement, **St Peter's Basilica** ❷⓺ (Basilica di San Pietro; www.vatican.va; free; no bare legs or shoulders) nevertheless suffers from the competing visions of its master architects – Bramante, Carlo Maderno, Michelangelo and Raphael among them – each of whom often worked with a pope peering over his shoulder.

From 1506, when the new basilica was begun under Julius II, until 1626 when it was consecrated, St Peter's Basilica changed form several times. It started out as a simple Greek cross, with four arms of equal length, as favoured by Bramante and Michelangelo, and ended up as Maderno's Latin cross, extended by a long nave, as demanded by the popes of the Counter-Reformation. One result is that Maderno's porticoed facade and nave obstruct a clear view of Michelangelo's dome from the square.

The basilica's finest treasure, Michelangelo's **Pietà** (1500), is in its own chapel. The artist was 25 when he executed this moving marble sculpture of the Virgin cradling the crucified Christ. It is the only work that he signed (on the ribbon that crosses the Madonna's breast), after overhearing people crediting it to another sculptor. Since the statue was attacked by a fanatic with a hammer in 1972

THE LEGACY OF POPE FRANCIS

Pope Francis, leader of the Catholic church from 2013 until his death in 2025, will be remembered as a progressive who put social and economic justice at the heart of his papacy. Born in Buenos Aires as Jorge Bergoglio, grandchild of Italian immigrants to Argentina, he studied chemistry before joining the Jesuit order to become a priest. In 2013, while cardinal archbishop of Buenos Aires, he was chosen as the successor to Benedict XVI, becoming Catholicism's first Jesuit pope, the first Latin American successor to Saint Peter, and first non-European leader in over a thousand years. Throughout his twelve years, the pontiff was a reformer with a forward-thinking influence on issues such as migration and the climate emergency. He was inclusive towards same-sex relationships. However, his tenure has not been without criticism. Though he fought to modernise the Catholic Church, this principle of equality was not extended to women within its own ranks. The Church's refusal to contemplate female ordination, as well as brushing off child sex abuse accusations, tainted Pope Francis's mission. Nonetheless, in an institution resistant to change, Pope Francis was a force for positive change in an unequal world. On 21 April 2025, Pope Francis died aged 88 from a stroke following double pneumonia.

(the damage was immediately restored), it has been protected by bulletproof glass. Reverence can also cause damage: on the thirteenth-century bronze statue of St Peter the toes of the right foot have been worn away by the lips and caressing fingers of pilgrims over the centuries.

Beneath the dome, Bernini's great *baldacchino* (canopy) soars over the high altar. The canopy and four spiralling columns were cast from bronze beams taken from the Pantheon. At the foot of each column a coat of arms bears the three bees of the Barberini Pope Urban VIII, who commissioned the work. In the apse is another extravagant Baroque work, Bernini's bronze and marble *Cathedra* ('Throne') *of St Peter*, into which the saint's wooden throne is supposedly incorporated. Also by Bernini is the tomb of Urban VIII.

For his imposing **dome**, Michelangelo drew inspiration from the Pantheon and Brunelleschi's cupola on Florence's cathedral. A lift takes you as far as the gallery above the nave, which gives a dizzying view down into the basilica, as well as close-ups of the inside of the dome. A succession of spiral stairs and ramps leads up to the outdoor balcony, which encircles the top of the dome for stunning views of St Peter's Square, the Vatican City and all of Rome.

The **Vatican Grottoes** beneath the basilica contain the tombs of popes and numerous little chapels. The **necropolis**, even deeper underground, shelters pre-Christian tombs, as well as a simple monument that marks St Peter's alleged burial place (booking required; www.necropolivaticana.org/en). Masses are said in the side chapels, in various languages.

The Vatican Museums

It should come as no surprise that the headquarters of the Roman Catholic Church – the world's greatest patron of painters, sculptors and architects – should have one of the world's richest art collections. At the **Vatican Museums** ㉗ (Musei Vaticani; www.

museivaticani.va), 7km (4 miles) of rooms and galleries offer a microcosm of Western civilisation. There is an utterly bewildering amount of items on display here; it is advisable to prioritise what you most want to see and skim the rest.

The fascinating **Museo Pio-Clementino** displays a wonderful collection of classical art salvaged from the ruthless dismantling of ancient monuments in the sixteenth century to make way for the Renaissance city. The most celebrated piece is the first century BC *Laocoön*

Giuseppe Momo's staircase

group: the Trojan priest and his two sons who were strangled by serpents sent by the goddess Athena for refusing to allow the Greek horse to enter Troy. Famous during Imperial times, it was unearthed from a vineyard on the Esquiline Hill in 1506, to the delight of Michelangelo, who rushed to view it. It now stands in a recess of the octagonal Belvedere Courtyard.

Roman copies of other Greek sculptures, such as the *Aphrodite of Cnidos* by Praxiteles and the *Apollo Belvedere*, achieved fame as great as the lost originals. In particular, note the powerful, muscular, first-century BC *Torso* by Apollonius, which has had a profound influence on artists and sculptors to this day.

The **Museo Etrusco** shelters the finds unearthed from a seventh-century BC Etruscan burial mound at Cerveteri (see page 97), whose tomb yielded an abundance of treasures. Among the fine

School of Athens, Stanza della Segnatura

jewellery is a gold brooch curiously decorated with lions and ducklings. Look out for the bronze statue of a sprightly Etruscan warrior, the *Mars of Todi*, from the fourth century BC.

Judging by the number of obelisks scattered throughout the city, Egyptian art was much sought after by the ancient Romans. The basis of the collection in the **Museo Egiziano** rests on finds from Rome and its environs, particularly from the Gardens of Sallust between the Pincian and Quirinal hills, the Temple of Isis on the Campus Martius and Hadrian's Villa at Tivoli (see page 93). One room recreates the underground chamber of a tomb in the Valley of the Kings.

The Raphael Rooms

Pope Julius II took a calculated risk in 1508 when he called in a relatively untried 26-year-old to decorate his new residence. The result was the four **Stanze di Raffaello** (the Raphael Rooms). In the central and most-visited Stanza della Segnatura are the two masterly frescoes, *Disputation over the Holy Sacrament* and the famous *School of Athens*, which contrasted theological and philosophical wisdom. The *Disputation* unites biblical figures with historical pillars of the faith such as Pope Gregory, Thomas Aquinas and others, including painter Fra Angelico and the divine Dante. At the centre of the *School*, Raphael is believed to have given red-robed Plato the features of Leonardo da Vinci, while portraying Michelangelo as the thoughtful Heraclitus, seated in the foreground. Raphael himself appears in the lower right-hand corner.

For a stark contrast to Raphael's grand manner, seek out the gentle beauty of Fra Angelico's frescoes in the **Cappella del Beato Angelico** (Chapel of Nicholas V). The lives of saints Lawrence and Stephen are told in delicately subdued pinks and blues, highlighted with gold.

The six richly decorated halls of the **Borgia Apartments** contain Pinturicchio's frescoes, with portraits of the Spanish Borgia Pope Alexander VI, and leads into the **Collection of Modern Religious Art** opened in 1973 by Paul VI. Among the twentieth-century works are Matisse's Madonna sketches, Rodin bronzes, Picasso ceramics, designs for ecclesiastical robes and, somewhat unexpectedly, a grotesque pope by Francis Bacon.

One of Europe's finest collections of ancient manuscripts and rare books is held in the **Apostolic Library**. In the great reading room, or Sistine Hall, designed by Domenico Fontana in 1588, walls and ceilings are covered with paintings of ancient libraries, conclaves, thinkers and writers. Showcases holding precious manuscripts have replaced the old lecterns. A 1600-year-old copy of Virgil's works, the poems of Petrarch, a sixth-century gospel of St Matthew and Henry VIII's love letters to Anne Boleyn are among the prized possessions.

The Sistine Chapel

Nothing can prepare you for the wonder of the **Sistine Chapel** (Cappella Sistina), built for Sixtus IV in the fifteenth century. Restored in a twenty-year project that finished in 1994, the brightness and freshness of the frescoes are overwhelmingly beautiful. At the time some art critics claimed that the frescoes had been cleaned beyond recognition and had lost their original tonality. Be that as it may, visitors seem to yield to the power of

The stunning Sistine Chapel

Michelangelo's ceiling and his *Last Judgement*. The other wall frescoes, by Botticelli, Ghirlandaio, Pinturicchio, Rosselli and Signorelli, are barely acknowledged. In this private papal chapel, where cardinals hold their conclaves to elect new popes, the glory of the Catholic Church achieves its finest artistic expression.

The chapel portrays the biblical story of man, in three parts: from Adam to Noah; the giving of the Law to Moses; and from the birth of Jesus to the Last Judgement. Towards the centre of the ceiling, you will be able to make out the celebrated outstretched finger of the *Creation of Adam*. Most overwhelming of all is the impression of the whole. This is best appreciated looking back from the bench by the chapel's exit.

On the chapel's altar wall is Michelangelo's tempestuous *Last Judgement*, finished 25 years after the ceiling's completion in 1512, when the artist was in his sixties. An almost-naked Jesus dispenses justice; he is more like a stern, classical god-hero than the conventionally gentle biblical figure. It is said that the artist's agonising self-portrait can be seen in the flayed skin of St Bartholomew, below Jesus.

The Picture Gallery

Amid all the Vatican's treasures, the fifteen rooms of the **Pinacoteca Vaticana** (Picture Gallery), in a separate wing, sometimes get short shrift. Covering nine centuries of painting, there are important works by Fra Angelico, Perugino, Raphael's *Transfiguration*, Leonardo da Vinci's unfinished *St Jerome*, Bellini's *Pietà* and Caravaggio's *Descent from the Cross*. As you wander the galleries, glance out of the windows to view St Peter's dome over the Vatican Gardens (the best views are from the Gallery of the Maps). Take a rest in the Cortile della Pigna, dominated by the bronze pine-cone fountain (first century AD) that gives the courtyard its name.

Trastevere, The Aventine and Testaccio

Highlights
- **Trastevere**, see page 82
- **The Aventine**, see page 83
- **Testaccio**, see page 84

The Ponte Fabricio, one of Rome's oldest bridges (62 BC), links the left bank to the tiny **Isola Tiberina** (Tiber Island). Three centuries before Christ the island was the sacred property of Aesculapius, god of healing, to whom a temple and hospital were dedicated. The large **Fatebenefratelli** hospital, originally founded in 1548 by the friars of St John of God, stands here to this day, occupying most of the island. A second bridge, Ponte Cestio, remodelled in the nineteenth century, leads over to the river's right bank and the neighbourhood of Trastevere.

Santa Maria in Trastevere apse

Trastevere

Trastevere means 'across the Tiber'; *Tevere* is the Italian for Tiber. Despite the gentrification commonly seen in formerly working-class areas of European cities which has dotted the district with smart shops and eateries, Trastevere retains a lively character all of its own, particularly in the cobbled streets around Piazza di Santa Maria in Trastevere. The church of **Santa Maria in Trastevere** ㉘ is reputedly the oldest in Rome; its foundation can be traced back to the third century AD, but the present structure dates from 1130–43 and is the work of Pope Innocent II, himself a *Trasteverino*. The facade is decorated with a beautiful thirteenth-century mosaic of the Virgin flanked by ten maidens bearing lamps. The highlights of the interior are undoubtedly the twelfth-century Byzantine mosaics covering the floor and apse.

Before entering **Santa Cecilia in Trastevere**, pause in the courtyard of the church to admire the russet Baroque facade and endearingly leaning Romanesque tower (AD 1113). Now regarded as the patron saint of music, St Cecilia was martyred for her Christian faith in AD 230. Her chapel stands over the site of her home and caldarium (the bathhouse, still visible), in which she was tortured by scalding and finally beheaded. The sculptor Stefano Maderno was on hand when her tomb was excavated in 1599, and his beautiful statue shows the miraculously conserved body that served as his model.

The **Museo di Roma in Trastevere** (www.museodiromaintrastevere.it; charge) is housed in a former Carmelite convent on Piazza di Sant'Egidio. A series of life-sized exhibits, including a chemist and an inn, represents the daily life of nineteenth-century Rome, and paintings, prints, drawings and watercolours reveal the changing face of the city and surrounding countryside, as seen by local and visiting artists.

The **Gianicolo** (Janiculum Hill) can be reached from Trastevere by following the long and winding Via Garibaldi uphill. After the liberation of Rome from papal rule in 1870, this hill became a gathering place where anticlerical citizens could honour Giuseppe Garibaldi. A large equestrian monument to the freedom-fighter stands on **Piazzale Garibaldi** ㉙ and, a little further north, is another for his wife, the intrepid Anita. The views from the terrace are magnificent. Also on the hill is **San Pietro in Montorio**, which contains works by Vasari, del Piombo and Bernini. Bramante's tiny **Tempietto**, one of the gems of the Renaissance, was erected in the courtyard in 1502.

The Aventine

Revered in ancient times as the 'Sacred Mount', when it stood outside Rome's walls, the Aventine Hill (Monte Aventino) remains a quiet sanctuary above the clamour of the city. An aristocratic district in the Imperial era, the hill is still a favoured residential zone, with villas and apartments set in shady gardens.

The Aventine is also the site of some of the earliest Christian churches, the most

> **NOTES**
>
> *Noantri*, Roman dialect for 'we others' or 'the rest of us', reflects the way the Trasteverini see themselves. It is also the name of their festival of music, food and fireworks in the last two weeks of July.

> **NOTES**
>
> Bramante's Tempietto is one of the finest examples of High Renaissance architecture. Set in an Early Renaissance courtyard, it possesses a gravity all of its own – marking the alleged site of St Peter's crucifixion.

beautiful of which is the basilica of **Santa Sabina** ㉚, built around AD 425. The 24 white Corinthian columns lining the nave give the church a classic harmony, while the beautiful carved fifth-century cypress-wood doors in the portico contain one of the earliest depictions of the crucifixion. Through an atrium window you can see a descendant of an orange tree planted by St Dominic in 1220. A few steps away stands the villa of the **Cavalieri di Malta** (Knights of Malta). Peep through the keyhole of the closed garden gates for a perfectly framed view of the dome of the distant St Peter's.

Testaccio

Just below the genteel residential slopes of the Aventine Hill lies the bustling neighbourhood of **Testaccio**, traditionally working class and now on the rise. The Mattatoio was a slaughterhouse until 1975, but these days part of the complex hosts a contemporary art museum (www.mattatoioroma.it; open during exhibitions only). Prestigious international exhibitions and installations take advantage of this unusual gallery space. There's a busy nightlife scene in Testaccio, with some of the most authentic *trattorie* in Rome and a growing array of chic wine bars and delis.

For something more tranquil, head to Porta San Paolo, where dark cypresses shade the beautiful **Cimitero Acattolico** ㉛ (Protestant Cemetery; www.cemeteryrome.it; free), where John Keats was buried in 1821 and where the ashes of his friend Shelley were interred the following year. Towering over the cemetery is Rome's only **pyramid** (Piramide di Caio Cestio), which has survived because it was incorporated in the city walls. A colonial magistrate, Caius Cestius, commissioned the 30-metre (100ft) monument for his tomb in 20 BC on his return from Egypt.

Monti and Esquilino

> **Highlights**
> - **Diocletian's Baths and Palazzo Massimo**, see page 86
> - **Santa Maria Maggiore**, see page 87
> - **San Giovanni in Laterano**, see page 87
> - **San Clemente**, see page 89

Sculpture of Saint Cecilia in Santa Cecilia in Trastevere

On the western side of the Esquiline Hill crouches the large *rione* (neighbourhood) of **Monti**, encompassing the Fori Imperiali and two major basilicas: Santa Maria Maggiore and San Giovanni in Laterano. The hilly, leafy streets between Via Panisperna and Via Cavour, have managed to retain interesting traces of their medieval past, at the same time as giving off an intimate village feel. On the other side of the hill is Piazza Vittorio Emanuele II, the focal point of the **Esquilino** rione, a multiethnic area with many diverse food shops and a local market

Niobid statue, Palazzo Massimo

selling fresh produce, spices, clothes and domestic goods on Via Lamarmora.

Diocletian's Baths and Palazzo Massimo

Part of the Museo Nazionale Romano, the **Terme di Diocleziano** ③② (www.museonazionaleromano.beniculturali.it; charge) offer a good introduction to Rome's Greek and Roman antiquities. Larger even than those of Caracalla, Diocletian's Baths covered 120 hectares (300 acres), part of which are now occupied by the Piazza della Repubblica and the church of Santa Maria degli Angeli, near the Termini station.

The largest part of the Museo Nazionale Romano collection is housed in the nearby nineteenth-century **Palazzo Massimo** (www.coopculture.it; charge), including frescoes taken from the imperial villa of Livia. These show nature at its most bountiful, with flowers, trees, birds and fruit painted with great attention to detail, but can only be visited as part of a guided tour. There is also an impressive collection of statues and busts of emperors, their relatives and lovers, and mythological creatures. Highlights include the *Niobid* statue from the Gardens of Sallust, the seated bronze *Pugilist* or Boxer, and the *Sleeping Hermaphroditus*. There are also displays of ancient Roman jewellery, as well as coins from the Republic and Imperial eras up until the Renaissance.

Santa Maria Maggiore

Southeast of the Piazza della Repubblica is the Basilica of **Santa Maria Maggiore** ③. According to a thirteenth-century legend, this largest and most splendid of all the churches dedicated to the Virgin Mary was built in the fourth century by Pope Liberius after a vision from the Virgin Mary. In fact, the church almost certainly dates from AD 420, and was completed soon afterwards by Pope Sixtus III.

Glittering **mosaics** enhance the perfect proportions of the interior. Above the forty ancient Ionic columns of the triple nave, a mosaic frieze portrays Old Testament scenes leading to the coming of Christ. The theme is continued in the gilded Byzantine-style mosaics on the triumphal arch, detailing the birth and the childhood of Jesus, and culminates in the magnificent thirteenth-century portrayal of Mary and Jesus enthroned in the apse behind the high altar. Inlaid red and green precious marbles pattern the floor in a style pioneered by Rome's illustrious Cosmati family of craftsmen during the twelfth century.

Just south of Via Cavour is the fifth-century **San Pietro in Vincoli** ③④, built as a sanctuary for the chains with which Herod bound St Peter in Palestine. It contains one of Michelangelo's greatest sculptures, *Moses*, which was intended for St Peter's as part of the sculptor's unsuccessful project for Julius II's tomb. *Moses* was going to be just one of forty figures adorning the tomb, but the plan was aborted when Julius decided he wanted Michelangelo to paint the Sistine Chapel instead.

San Giovanni in Laterano

Situated in a large piazza to the southeast of the

> **NOTES**
>
> Outside San Giovanni in Laterano stands an obelisk brought from the Temple of Ammon in Thebes. It is the tallest in the world – 32 metres (102ft) – and, dating from the fifteenth century BC, very possibly the oldest of the thirteen still remaining in Rome.

The Basilica of San Clemente

Colosseum is the mother church of the Roman Catholic world (seat of the Pope as Bishop of Rome), **San Giovanni in Laterano** ㉟, which predated the first St Peter's Basilica by a few years. Popes lived in the Lateran Palace for a thousand years until they moved to Avignon, and then to the Vatican on their return in 1377. Fire, earthquake and looting by Vandals reduced the church to ruins over the centuries. The present structure uses the bronze central doors that once graced the entrance to the Curia in the Forum in ancient Rome. High above the basilica's facade, fifteen giant white statues of Jesus, John the Baptist and Church sages stand against the sky.

Transformed by Borromini in the seventeenth century, the sombre interior is more restrained than is usual for Baroque architects. The only exuberant touches are the coloured marble inlays of the paving and statues of the Apostles. The **baptistery**, site of the first Christian baptism in Rome, preserves some fifth- to seventh-century mosaics. Brothers Jacopo and Pietro Vassalletto excelled themselves in the **cloisters**, where alternating straight and twisted columns, in mosaic style, are a perfect setting for some quiet meditation.

An ancient edifice opposite the basilica – almost all that's left of the original Lateran Palace – shelters the **Scala Santa**, the stairway brought back by St Helena from Jerusalem and said to have been trodden by Jesus in the house of Pontius Pilate. The devout still climb the 28 marble steps to the **Sancta Sanctorum** ('Holy of Holies', the private chapel of the popes; charge) on their knees.

A free musical festival called is held every year outside San Giovanni on the first of May.

San Clemente

On the Via San Giovanni in Laterano stands a gem of a church, which hides a fascinating history within its three levels. In its present basilica form, **San Clemente** ❸ (www.basilicasanclemente.com) dates from the twelfth century, with three naves divided by ancient columns and embellished by a pavement of geometric designs. A symbolic mosaic in the apse features the Cross as the Tree of Life nourishing all living things: birds, animals and plants. To the right of the nave, a staircase leads down to the fourth-century **basilica**, which underpins the present church. The Romanesque frescoes, unfortunately, have drastically faded, but copies show the near-perfect condition in which they were uncovered early in the twentieth century.

An ancient stairway leads deeper underground to a maze of corridors and chambers, believed to be the home of St Clement himself, third successor to St Peter as Pope and martyred by Hadrian in AD 88. Also here is the earliest religious structure on the site, a second-century AD pagan **temple** *(Mithraeum)* dedicated to the god Mithras.

Further afield

Highlights
- **Via Appia Antica**, see page 90
- **The catacombs**, see page 91
- **Ostiense**, see page 92

The Old Appian Way

Via Appia Antica

Don't miss a visit to the **Via Appia Antica** ③, the Old Appian Way, just outside the city walls. Heading southeast through the Porta San Sebastiano, look back for a good view of the old **Aurelian Wall**, still enclosing part of Rome. Its massive defensive ramparts stretch into the distance, topped by towers and bastions built to resist the onslaught of Barbarian invasions in the third century. Ahead lies a narrow lane, hemmed in at first by hedges and the high walls of film stars' and millionaires' homes – the Old Appian Way. When the Censor Appius Claudius opened the consular road and gave it his name in 312 BC, the Appian Way was the first of the great Roman roads. You can still see some of the original paving stones over which the Roman legions marched 370km (222 miles) on their way to Brindisi to set sail for the Levant and North Africa.

By law, burials could not take place within the city walls, so on either side of the road lie the ruins of sepulchres of twenty generations of patrician Roman families, some with simple tablets, others with impressive mausoleums.

At a fork in the road, the seventeenth-century chapel of **Domine Quo Vadis** marks the spot where St Peter, fleeing Nero's persecution, is said to have met Christ and asked: *'Domine, quo vadis?'* ('Whither goest thou, Lord?'). Christ is believed to have replied: 'I go to Rome to be crucified again.' Ashamed of his fear, Peter turned back to Rome and his own crucifixion.

The catacombs

Further along the Appia Antica, within a short distance of each other, are three of Rome's most celebrated **catacombs**: Domitilla, San Callisto (the largest and the most famous) and San Sebastiano. Millions of early Christians, among them many martyrs and saints, were buried in fifty of these vast underground cemeteries. Guides accompany groups into a labyrinth of damp, musty-smelling tunnels and chambers burrowed into the soft volcanic tufa rock, sometimes six levels deep. Early Christian paintings and carvings adorn the walls.

The **Catacombs of Domitilla** are the oldest and perhaps the most enjoyable to visit (www.catacombedomitilla.it; closed mid-Dec to mid-Jan; charge). These are the most extensive catacombs, and the only ones still to contain bones, and have the additional attraction of an entrance that goes through a sunken fourth-century church. The entrance to the **Catacombs of San Callisto** lies at the end of an avenue of cypresses (www.catacombe.roma.it; closed Feb; charge). An official tour takes you down to the second level of excavations, where you will see the burial niches, or *loculi*, cut into the rock one above the other on either side of the dark galleries. Occasionally, the narrow passages open out into larger chambers, or *cubicula*, where a family would be buried together. More than ten early popes were buried here. In the **Catacombs of San Sebastiano** (www.catacombe.org; closed Dec; charge), the bodies of the apostles Peter and Paul are said to have been hidden during the third-century persecutions.

Near the Catacombs of San Callisto is the poignant memorial of **Fosse Ardeatine**, a place of pilgrimage for modern Italians. In March 1944, in retaliation for the killing of 32 German soldiers by the Italian Resistance, the Nazis rounded up at random 335 Italian men (ten for each German and an extra fifteen for good measure) and machine-gunned them in the sandpits of the Via Ardeatina.

The cylindrical **Tomb of Cecilia Metella** (www.parcoarcheologicoappiaantica.it; charge) dominates the Appian landscape. This noblewoman was the wife of the immensely rich Crassus, who financed Julius Caesar's early campaigns. The well-preserved **Circus of Maxentius**, built for chariot races in AD 309, extends alongside.

Further south (entrance at Via Appia Nuova 1092) is the second-century **Villa dei Quintili** (www.parcoarcheologicoappiaantica.it; charge), the Quintili brothers' sumptuous residence, with a bath complex and nymphaeum, and the **Parco degli Acquedotti**, dotted with the remains of Roman aqueducts.

The Circus of Maxentius

Ostiense

South of Testaccio lie the Ostiense and Garbatella quarters, filled with striking late nineteenth- and early twentieth-century workers' apartment blocks. Once industrial, Ostiense is becoming more gentrified, offering some of Rome's hippest nightlife.

In a former electricity power plant, a ten-minute walk from Testaccio's pyramid, is one of Rome's must-see sights for all ages. The **Centrale Montemartini** (Via Ostiense 106; www.centralemontemartini.org; charge) has been converted into a fascinating museum that juxtaposes industrial machinery with more than four hundred classic Roman statues.

Between Via Guglielmo Marconi and the Tiber is **San Paolo Fuori le Mura**. Originally built by Constantine in AD 314 and enlarged by Valentinian II and Theodosius, St Paul's was Rome's largest church after St Peter's. It stood intact until razed by fire in 1823, but was faithfully restored. Massive Byzantine doors in eleventh-century bronze panels survived the fire and now appear on the west wall. A **ciborium** (1285) attributed to the Florentine architect and sculptor Arnolfo di Cambio decorates the high altar, under which lies the supposed burial place of St Paul the Apostle. Above the 86 Venetian marble columns runs a row of mosaic medallions representing all the popes, from St Peter to the present day. A main feature is the peaceful Benedictine cloister from the early thirteenth century.

Excursions

Highlights
- **Tivoli and the Sabine Hills**, see page 93
- **Ostia Antica**, see page 95
- **Cerveteri**, see page 97

Tivoli and the Sabine Hills

The picturesque town of **Tivoli** perches on a steep slope amid the **Sabine Hills**. Inhabited even in ancient times, when it was known as *Tibur*, Tivoli prospered throughout the Middle Ages. It preserves interesting Roman remains, as well as medieval churches and its famous Renaissance villa. Cotral buses (www.cotralspa.it) connect Rome to Tivoli from the Ponte Mammolo metro station (line B). Not all the buses stop at Villa Adriana. By car, the drive takes 45 minutes on Via Tiburtina; or take the A4 Autostrada towards Aquila and exit at Tivoli.

Villa d'Este, Villa Adriana and Villa Gregoriana

The **Villa d'Este** ❸ (https://villae.cultura.gov.it; charge) sprawls along the hillside. From its balconies, view the fabled gardens falling away in a series of terraces – a paradise of cypresses, umbrella pines, fountains (some five hundred) and statues. Cardinal Ippolito II d'Este conceived this modest villa and garden in 1550; architect Piero Ligorio created it. On the **Viale delle Cento Fontane** water jets splash into a basin guarded stone eagles. The **Fontana dell'Organo**, originally accompanied by organ music, cascades down the rocks.

Five kilometres (3 miles) down the road, tucked away at the foot of the hills, lie the ruins of **Villa Adriana** ❹ (Hadrian's Villa; https://villae.cultura.gov.it; charge). Spread over 70 hectares (173 acres), this retirement hideaway of the Emperor Hadrian was one of the most extravagant of such projects in ancient times. You enter the ruins through the colonnades of the Greek-style **Pecile** (a pool once surrounded by a portico), which leads to the imperial residence. Adjoining the palace are guest rooms, their mosaic floors visible, and an underground passageway through which servants moved about. The **Teatro Marittimo**, a pavilion surrounded by a reflecting pool and circular portico, epitomises the magic of the place. To the south, remnants

> **NOTES**
>
> Beyond the ancient and modern city, a 'Third Rome' exists 5km (3 miles) south along the Ostian Way. A complex of massive white-marble buildings, EUR was designed for a world fair in 1942 to mark twenty years of Fascism. War halted construction, and the fair never took place. EUR is now a thriving township of government ministries, offices and an array of museums including the Museum of Roman Civilization (www.museociviltaromana.it; currently closed for restoration) and the Museum of Civilizations (www.museodellecivilta.it; charge), which houses an ethnographic collection.

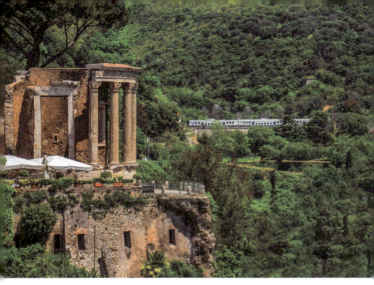

Temple of Vesta at Villa Gregoriana

of arches and copies of Greek-style caryatids surround the **Pool of Canopus** leading to the sanctuary of the Egyptian god Serapis.

Villa Gregoriana (https://fondoambiente.it/parco-villa-gregoriana-eng; charge), in the centre of Tivoli, is an oasis of waterfalls, ravines and grottoes. In 1826 the River Aniene burst its banks and swept away much of the town. Architect Clemente Folchi duly diverted the river, boring into the mountainside to create a series of spectacular waterfalls. Colour-coded walks lead off from the main waterfall, ending up at the **Temple of Vesta**, a round, travertine structure dating back to the first century BC.

Ostia Antica

Some people argue that the ruins of Ostia Antica rival those at Pompeii, though they're much less famous and less crowded.

Excavations continue to uncover fascinating sections of the former seaport and naval base of Rome from when it was the most important city in the Western world. The long-buried city of Ostia stands at the mouth of the Tiber, 23km (14 miles) southwest of the capital on the shores of the Tyrrhenian Sea. Sea-faring vessels were unable to travel inland along the shallow Tiber, so river barges plied back and forth from the port, carrying imperial Rome's supply of food and building materials. During its heyday, the port city had 100,000 residents, two splendid public baths, a theatre (where plays are still occasionally offered), many temples and wealthy villas.

The ruins of **Ostia Antica** ❹ (www.ostiaantica.beniculturali.it; charge), set among cypresses and pines (perfect for picnics), may reveal more about daily life and the building methods of ancient Rome than those of the capital do. Excavations since the nineteenth century have unearthed **Decumanus Maximus** (Main Street) and a grid of side streets, which visitors are able to roam freely. The **Piazzale delle Corporazioni** (Square of the Guilds) housed seventy commercial offices around a porticoed central temple to Ceres, goddess of agriculture. Mosaic mottoes and emblems in the pavement tell of the trading of grain factors, caulkers, ropemakers and shipowners from all over the world. The **theatre** next door, built by Agrippa, is worth the climb up the tiered seats for a view over the whole ruined city.

As in Rome, the **Forum** was the focus of city life, dominated at one end by the Capitol, a temple dedicated to Jupiter, Juno and Minerva, and at the other by the Temple of Rome and Augustus, with the Curia (seat of the municipal authorities) and the basilica, or law courts, lying in between. To see a typical residence, visit the **House of Cupid and Psyche** with its rooms paved in marble and built round a central garden courtyard. Nearby, a small on-site museum traces Ostia's history through statues, busts and frescoes.

The 1930s resort of **Lido di Ostia** attracts weekending Romans. The sea is not very clean here, but it is lined with *stabilimenti*

Ostia Antica

(beach clubs), many of which have restaurants and pools. There are some sections of *spiaggia libera* ('free beach', without a fee) and at night bars open up on the beach.

Cerveteri

The **Etruscan necropolis** at **Cerveteri** ㊶, 43km (27 miles) northwest of Rome, was known as *Caere*, one of the twelve towns of the powerful Etruscan League, which declined in the third century BC after becoming a Roman dependency (www.tarquinia-cerveteri.it; charge). The scores of **tombs** here represent every kind of burial, dating from the seventh to first century BC. Decorations and carvings depict the things that Etruscans felt they needed in the afterlife. The **Museo Nazionale Cerite**, housed in a sixteenth-century castle in Piazza Santa Maria, displays a collection of objects from the tombs.

Rome: a centre of fashion and design

Things to do

Culture

Rome is not only rich in culture, but the city knows how to put on a damn good show, from classical music in historic settings such as the Campidoglio to ballet performances against evocative backdrops like the Baths of Caracalla. Music venues run the gamut of jazz, blues, folk, rock, reggae and salsa, while hip bars and late-night clubs keep the party going til dawn.

Classical music, ballet and opera

One of the best venues for classical and contemporary music is the **Auditorium Parco della Musica** (Viale Pietro de Coubertin 30; www.auditorium.com), with a large outdoor amphitheatre, three indoor halls and exhibition spaces. Bus #910 runs from Stazione Termini to the Auditorium. The renowned **Accademia di Santa Cecilia** (www.santacecilia.it) and its symphonic and chamber orchestras host their main concerts at the Auditorium from October to May.

Classical music is also performed in historic settings, such as the **Campidoglio** (see page 34), the beautifully frescoed **Oratorio del Gonfalone** and the cloister of **Santa Maria della Pace**. Outdoor venues include Villa Ada, Teatro di Marcello and Villa Celimontana.

Opera and ballet

Opera and ballet performances are presented at the **Teatro dell'Opera** (Piazza Beniamino Gigli near Via Torino; www.operaroma.it). The opera season runs from November to late spring, with ballet the rest of the year.

In the months of July and August, the troupe perform a selection of operas and ballets outdoors in the highly evocative setting of the **Baths of Caracalla**.

Music venues

Music clubs abound, from jazz, blues and folk to rock, reggae and salsa. A major live venue is **Atlantico Live** (Viale dell'Oceano Atlantico 271D; www.atlanticoroma.it). Blues and jazz can be found at **Alexanderplatz** (Via Ostia 9; www.alexanderplatzjazz.com) and **Casa del Jazz** (Via di Porta Ardeatina 55; www.casadeljazz.com). **Klang** (Via Stefano Colonna 9; www.klangroma.com) also hosts free live music events (mostly electronic) every evening between Thursday and Sunday; there's a globally inspired menu and a weekly changing craft-beer roster.

Finally, **MONK** (Via Giuseppe Mirri 35; www.monkroma.it) is an outdoor events venue that often hosts live music, and includes a theatre, children's play area, basketball hoops, a bar and street food stalls.

Cinema

Cinemas usually show foreign films dubbed into Italian. The exception is the **Nuovo Olimpia** (near the Spanish Steps; www.circuitocinema.com/cinema/cinema-nuovo-olimpia-roma).

Look for the 'V.O.' (versione originale) label on a local paper's movie listings.

Nightlife

Nightlife in Rome used to be limited to **Testaccio** on the south side of town near Piramide. The area continues to expand, stretching toward **Via Ostiense**, and attracts a varied, if mostly younger, crowd. The modern suburb of **EUR** is peppered with popular nightclubs, often hosting visiting DJs. In the summer, the beach clubs in **Ostia** morph into dance clubs, often offering live music. The **Centre** is more about wine bars and sophisticated clientele.

Spazio 900 in EUR (Viale Marconi 26/b; www.spazionovecento.it) is a bastion for special events: DJs from Ibiza frequently moonlight here. Nearby, the famous DJs at **Goa** (Via Libetta 13; www.

goaclub.com/goa-club/goa-club) keep locals up until dawn with electro and house beats. A very hip hangout is **Caffé Propaganda** (Via Claudia 15; www.caffepropaganda.it), serving great drinks to a cosmopolitan crowd in a sumptuous turn-of-the-century interior.

In Trastevere, popular **Bar Santo Calisto** (Piazza di S. Calisto 3) has a relaxing atmosphere and incredibly cheap drinks. Other hip bars include **Doney** (Via Veneto 141; www.restaurantdoney.com/it), a 1960s-era cocktail bar that has had a number of refits over the years and still attracts the cool set. If you like combination of chocolate and alcohol, **Cioccolata e Vino** (Vicolo del Cinque 31a) is a must; shots with suggestive names are served in chocolate cups by entertaining and friendly staff.

Teatro dell'Opera hosts opera and ballet

Shopping

Italian fashion and artisan products are extremely popular and it's not unusual for visitors to buy an extra suitcase to take home goodies. The small, traditional shops are fun to browse, and real bargains can be found in the January and July sales.

IVA (value-added tax) is incorporated into prices on a sliding scale, reaching 22 percent. Non-EU citizens are entitled to a refund of this tax on purchases of €155 or more, if made in one place; ask for an invoice from the seller. Save receipts until you leave your last EU destination. If you are departing from Rome, take your receipts to be stamped before you check in. For more information, visit www.globalblue.com.

EUR, a clubbing district

Where to shop

The most fashionable (and expensive) shopping district lies between Piazza di Spagna and Via del Corso. The best in high fashion, jewellery, fabrics and leather is available in elegant shops on **Via dei Condotti** and its side streets: **Via Borgognona**, **Via Frattina** and **Via Bocca di Leone**. Stroll from Piazza di Spagna to **Piazza del Popolo** on Via del Babuino for other famous-name boutiques. Streets branching from Campo de' Fiori are good for quirky fashion and artisans' boutiques and workshops.

Via Cola di Rienzo, just across the river, is not so exclusive but its stores offer high quality. **Via Nazionale** and **Via del Tritone** are cheaper places to pick up clothes and leather.

The best of Rome's few big stores are Coin (Piazzale Appio, near San Giovanni in Laterano and Termini Station) and La Rinascente (inside the Galleria Alberto Sordi on Piazza Colonna and another branch on Piazza Fiume). The OVS (Oviesse) and Upim chains are good for essentials.

Be prepared to haggle at **Porta Portese**, Rome's famous flea market held on Sunday morning in tiny streets parallel to Viale Trastevere between Porta Portese and Piazza Ippolito Nievo in Trastevere. Here you will find clothes, furniture, bric-a-brac, jewellery and books.

The outdoor market in **Via Sannio** (near San Giovanni in Laterano) has bargain clothes. Between Via G. Pepe and Via Mamiani, in former barracks, is **Nuovo Mercato Esquilino**, Rome's colourful and multicultural food and clothes market.

What to buy

Antiques. Dealers by the score sell exquisite (but expensive) silver, glass, porcelain, furniture and paintings. The best shops are on Via del Babuino and Via Margutta (between the Spanish Steps and the Piazza del Popolo), Via Giulia (behind Palazzo Farnese) and Via dei Coronari (near Piazza Navona). Make sure to buy only from a reputable dealer, who will provide a certificate of guarantee and obtain a government export permit.

Books and prints. The open-air Mercato delle Stampe at Largo Fontanella Borghese (off Via del Corso, daily 7am–1pm) specialises in prints and books.

Ceramics. Modigliani (Via Frattina 56; www.modigliani.it) has a wealth of design-led handcrafted and hand-painted ceramics.

Fashion. All the famous names of Italian *alta moda* (high fashion) are represented in the Piazza di Spagna area. Fendi and Valentino

Street stalls

are Rome's local stars, but you'll find all their peers as well: Armani, Prada, Missoni, Gucci, Laura Biagiotti, and Max Mara.

Food and wine. Gourmand delicacies include Parmesan, salami, Parma and San Daniele ham (*prosciutto crudo* – meat products cannot be taken to the US), extra virgin olive oil, Castelli Romani wines and fiery *grappa*. Trimani (Via Goito 20; www.trimani.com) is the city's most historic wine shop, open since 1821, located in the Jewish Ghetto. Beppe e i suoi formaggi offers a variety of locally made cheeses and cold cuts (Via Santa Maria del Pianto 9A; www.beppeeisuoiformaggi.it), while Volpetti (Via Marmorata 47; www.volpetti.com) sells gourmet Italian delicacies and specialises in cured meats.

Interior design. Atelier Monti (Via Panisperna 42; www.ateliermonti.it), close to the Colosseum, displays high-spec home

furnishings. For the latest in lighting head to Artemide (Via Pisanelli 1; www.artemide.it) and Flos (Via del Babuino 84; www.flos.com).
Jewellery. You'll find modern, antique and costume jewellery in Rome. Try Bulgari in Via dei Condotti for opulence, or the stores on Via del Governo Vecchio – particularly Tempi Moderni (No. 108) – for vintage and costume jewellery.
Leather. Stylish shoes, handbags, gloves, wallets and luggage abound. Furla (www.furla.com), on Piazza di Spagna, sells fashionable and affordable bags.

Sports and activities

Romans have been passionate about spectator sports since the ancient times. These days, most major sporting events take place in the **Stadio Olimpico**, which has been home to the **AS Roma** (www.asroma.com) and **SS Lazio** (www.sslazio.it) teams – both in Italy's Serie A – since the 1950s.

The Stadio Olimpico also hosts two of the **Six Nations Rugby** games every year (www.sixnationsrugby.com). Not too far away, the **Foro Italico** is home to all tennis, swimming and athletics competitions, while Rome's **PalaLottomatica** stadium in EUR seats over 11,000 basketball fans and hosts all Virtus Roma home games.

Every year in late May, the four-day **International Horse Show** in Piazza di (www.piazzadisiena.it) features top international riders, as well as thrilling showjumping and polo matches.

Rome for children

As a general rule, Italians love children, and there are plenty of things to keep young ones entertained in the capital. Kids are usually fascinated by Rome's fountains, the **Bocca della Verità** (see page 57) and, for the braver souls, the underground **catacombs** (see page 91).

On Piazza Navona there are all sorts of performers and entertainers who will stoke the imagination of young minds.

Gelato: a winner with kids

Another favourite is the **Villa Borghese park** (see page 66), where kids can take pony rides, ride the merry-go-round (near Porta Pinciana), bicycle and rollerblade (hire kiosk near the Pincio), and glide across the boating lake (near Piazza di Siena). Rome's zoo is also tucked away in a corner and now referred to as **Bioparco** (www.bioparco.it) due to its animal-friendly outlook.

For the under-12s, the children's museum, **Explora** (www.mdbr.it), is at Via Flaminia 82, a ten-minute walk from Piazza del Popolo. Laid out like a small city with a supermarket, a farm, a bank and a water circuit, it's a place where children can touch, observe and play.

Festivals and events

1 January New Year's Day. Public holiday.
6 January *Befana* (Epiphany). Lively festival held in Piazza Navona. Public holiday.
February/March *Carnevale*. Masked processions and parades.
9 March *Festa di Santa Francesca Romana*. Blessing of cars by the patron saint of motorists, Monastero Oblate di Santa Francesca Romana, Via Teatro di Marcello 32.
March/April Easter weekend. Pope leads the Stations of the Cross (*Via Crucis*) on Good Friday at the candlelit Colosseum. On Easter Sunday the Pope blesses the crowds from the balcony of St Peter's

at noon. Easter Monday is a public holiday when many Italians barbecue outside with friends and family.

April–May *Festa della Primavera*. Spring Festival, azaleas on the Spanish Steps.

21 April Anniversary of the legendary founding of Rome, celebrated with an evening of fireworks.

25 April Liberation Day. Public holiday.

1 May *Festa del Lavoro*. Labour Day, free rock concert usually held in the square in front of the basilica of San Giovanni in Laterano. Public holiday.

June Rome Pride, which includes a lively parade and street parties in Via San Giovanni in Laterano, usually takes place on the second weekend of June.

2 June *Republic Day*, with parades on Via dei Fori Imperiali. Public holiday.

29 June *Festa di San Pietro e San Paolo*. Solemn rites in St Peter's Square.

July–August *Estate Romana*. The 'Roman Summer' brings together a wealth of events, from concerts to outdoor film festivals.

July *Festa de' Noantri*. Two-week long festival in Trastevere with music, food, street theatre, stalls and fireworks.

5 August *Festa della Madonna della Neve* in Santa Maria Maggiore.

15 August *Ferragosto* (Feast of the Assumption). Public holiday.

October *I Cento Pittori di Via Margutta*. Five-day open-air art exhibition in Via Margutta.

1 November *Ognissanti* (All Saints' Day). Public holiday.

2 November All Souls' Day. Romans visit family graves.

December Christmas market and fair set up on Piazza Navona (until 6 January).

8 December *Festa dell'Immacolata Concezione*. Public holiday.

24–26 December Christmas Eve midnight Mass celebrated by the Pope in St Peter's Basilica. 25 and 26 December are Christmas holidays.

Food and drink

For Italians, sitting down at the table and enjoying a meal together is always a celebration. It is normal to spend hours at the table, chatting with family and friends and drinking wine. The areas around Campo de' Fiori (see page 54) and nearby Piazza Navona (see page 50) are nowadays what the Via Veneto was during the days of *la dolce vita* – places to while away the evening, first at one of the many restaurants and later at an outdoor café. Other dining enclaves are Trastevere (see page 82) and the old Jewish Ghetto (see page 55), as well as Monti. But no matter where you are in Rome, it won't be hard to find a good pizzeria, a *trattoria* serving local dishes, or a "bar" serving delicious sandwiches for a quick lunch.

Coffee and a pastry, a typical Roman breakfast

Authentic Roman cuisine has its roots in *la cucina povera*, which translates as 'the poor man's cooking'. The Italian cooking style originated from the rural peasant class and was born out of necessity: it is defined by resourcefulness and creativity – making the most out of ingredients. You will find simple, traditional dishes, such as sautéed vegetables, chicken *cacciatore* (stew) and unfussy pastas and soups, not only in most *trattorias* but also in the city's

> ### SALUTI!
>
> Come dusk, Romans love to get together for an *aperitivo* – an alcoholic drink, often a glass of wine or a cocktail like an Aperol spritz, accompanied by a buffet that can include all kinds of pasta, salads, cheeses and meats. Many bars in town serve *aperitivo* buffets, but the most copious ones are in the centre, especially in Trastevere and around Piazza Navona.

more refined and expensive restaurants. Offal, also referred to as the cow's 'fifth quarter', is an essential part of Roman cuisine. These are the cuts of the butchered animal that once remained unclaimed after the prized cuts had been sold to the upper classes and include anything from tripe and tongue to heart and lung. Romans have created a whole cuisine around these cuts, and these dishes are still a core part of the nation's culinary identity to this day. You'll find *trippa* (tripe), *pajata* (suckling kid or lamb intestines), *coratella* (heart and lung), and *coda alla vaccinara* (oxtail in tomato sauce) on many restaurant menus, often accompanied by a variety of fresh vegetables, served raw or sautéed *(ripassate)* in a pan with garlic and olive oil.

Rome's dining scene also has a more adventurous side, with many restaurants offering creative reinterpretations of local dishes. One very successful new trend is the *trapizzino*, a pizza pocket stuffed with a small portion of popular Roman and Italian dishes. The city, too, has its fair share of decent international restaurants, but like everywhere else in Italy, the main focus remains on national cuisine.

When it comes to drinks, most restaurants offer the house wine, red or white, in quarter-, half- or one-litre carafes, as well as a decent array of bottled vintages. Rome's local wine comes from the surrounding province of Lazio. The whites from the Alban Hills, called Castelli Romani, are light and pleasant and can be sweet or dry. The most famous is Frascati. From further afield, the Chiantis of Tuscany are widely available, as are the velvety Valpolicella from the Veneto and Piedmont's full-bodied Barolo. Look out for the unusual Est! Est!! Est!!! from Montefiascone on Lake Bolsena.

Italian beer is tasty but usually not as strong as north European brands. Peroni, Nastro Azzurro and Moretti are national favourites, though craft beer is having somewhat of a moment in Rome too, and you won't have to look far to find an interesting brew. After dinner, try a glass of *grappa*, distilled from grapes, or icy *limoncello*, a lemon liqueur often served on the house.

Dessert often means *gelato*, or ice cream. It's usually better in an ice-cream parlour *(gelateria)* than in the average *trattoria*. Also delicious is the famous coffee-flavoured *tiramisù* (which literally means 'pick me up').

Classic carbonara

Top 10 things to try

1. Tonnarelli cacio e pepe

One of Rome's most popular pasta dishes, *tonnarelli cacio e pepe* is a type of thick, home-made egg spaghetti tossed in a creamy sauce of pecorino Romano cheese, sprinkled with lots of pepper. The ingredients are simple, but the perfect *cacio e pepe* requires culinary skill: in order to achieve the defining creaminess, it's important to find the right balance between the starchy pasta water and the grated pecorino.

> **NOTES**
>
> The restaurant bill will usually include service (called either *servizio* or *coperto*), but ask if you're not sure. It is customary (and polite) to leave a small tip, rounding up to the next euro or two.

2. Jewish-style artichokes

The ultimate staple of Roman-Jewish cuisine is the humble artichoke, first tenderised and opened like a flower, then deep-fried until golden and crispy, before a liberal salting. The best away to savour the tasty morsel is to first bite the soft part of the petals, then discard the harder edges, and finally eat the heart with knife and fork. Another must-try dish showcasing this unassuming vegetable is *carciofi alla romana,* pan-braised artichokes stuffed with mint, garlic, and parsley.

3. Puntarelle

Once only found in the Rome region, *puntarelle* have now taken Italy by storm and are available in supermarkets across the country. This Roman salad consists of an elongated variant of chicory shoots, sliced and soaked in water and lemon until they curl. The shoots, which are crunchy and slightly bitter, are then served with a dressing of vinegar, garlic, salt, anchovy and olive oil.

4. Offal

A staple of Roman cuisine (see page 109), offal comes in many forms, from liver to heart and tongue. The most popular dish, however, is *trippa*, or tripe, simmered in a tomato sauce spiked with local mint and enriched with pecorino Romano. Another must-try is oxtail, cooked with tomatoes, wine, carrots, onions and celery for five hours until it turns into a tender stew. You'll find these cuts at most traditional *trattorias*.

Trippa (tripe), a Roman staple

5. Cicoria ripassata

Romans sure love their veg, and it's rare to see a local eat a meal without a vegetable side dish. The most popular is *cicoria ripassata*, or sautéed chicory, a bitter green leafy vegetable from the dandelion family, fried with garlic and chili, and normally served with meat.

6. Carbonara

You can't say you've been to Rome if you haven't feasted on a plate of carbonara, a classic dish of spaghetti in a creamy sauce made from raw beaten eggs, *guanciale* (cured pork), pecorino Romano cheese and black pepper. Carbonara's famous cousin is *amatriciana,* a similar recipe that uses tomatoes instead of eggs.

7. Fiori fritti

The Roman appetiser par excellence, and a must before every pizza, is simply a courgette flower stuffed with mozzarella and anchovy and fried in a yeast-free batter until puffy and crunchy.

8. Saltimbocca alla Romana

The Italian name of these veal scallops literally means 'jump in the mouth', which is a fitting description considering how appetising they are. The meat slices are rolled in *prosciutto crudo* and cooked in sage, butter and flour, with a few drops of white wine.

9. Trapizzino

Since Italian chef Stefano Callegari invented this pizza pocket in 2008, it has become a popular street food all over Italy and beyond. Think a doughy triangle filled with all the most famous Roman and Italian dishes, from anchovy and stracchino cheese to eggplant parmigiana or chicken *cacciatore*.

10. Maritozzi

An airy and puffy brioche-like bun filled with whipped cream, often enriched with pine nuts or candied fruit. The name, which is an affectionate term for 'husband', recalls a century-old Roman tradition: young men once used *maritozzi* to conceal engagement rings, and offered them to their beloved to propose.

Where to eat

Some hotels, usually the larger ones, serve an English-style breakfast. Otherwise, head to any local bar or café and ask for a *caffè* (espresso) or cappuccino (with foaming hot milk), accompanied by a *cornetto* (croissant). You should order and pay at the till before taking the receipt to the barista, who will make your drink for you. Coffee is usually consumed standing up at the bar *(al banco)* in a few quick gulps; in the city centre and the more touristy areas you will pay extra if you sit down and are given waiter service.

For a quick snack at lunchtime, choose a *tavola calda*, a bar with informal tables serving a variety of hot and cold dishes to take away or eat on the spot. Many bars offer the *tramezzino* – half a sandwich on crustless loaf bread containing fillings like tuna,

> **NOTES**
>
> There are said to be as many forms of Italian pasta as there are French cheeses – over six hundred at the last count, with new ones created every year. Each sauce – tomato, cheese, meat or fish – needs its own noodle.

Eating out is part of the social tapestry of Roman life

chicken or egg salad, *prosciutto* or smoked salmon. Alternatively, order a sandwich at a local delicatessen *(alimentari)*; ask for a *panino ripieno*, a bread roll filled with the ingredients of your choice. You'll find street food all over town, either in the form of small shops selling fried cod or vegetables, pizza *al taglio* or sandwiches, or sometimes as market stands in the bigger food markets.

In theory, a *ristorante* is usually larger and more elaborate than the cosier *trattoria* or rustic *osteria*, but in Rome the distinction is often blurred. Price should not be taken as an indication of quality of cuisine – an expensive restaurant may offer a superb meal with service to match, but often you pay for the location. Venture just a few streets away from the famous tourist spots such as Piazza del Popolo and Piazza Navona, and you'll discover *trattorias* with lower prices, more appealing ambience and arguably better food with real character. Some restaurants offer fixed-price, three-course meals (*menù turistico* or *prezzo fisso*), which will save money, but you almost always get better food by ordering individual dishes.

Opening times

Roman restaurants generally serve lunch from 12.30pm until 3pm and dinner 8pm until 11pm. Some offer late-night supper and are open until 1 or 2am, but on the whole you'll be hard-pressed to find places serving meals outside the main times. They are usually closed one day a week, often Sunday or Monday. Try to book by phone, especially for peak hours (1.30pm and 9pm) and days (Friday and Saturday). From mid-August many restaurants close for up to four weeks, as Romans head out of town for their annual holidays.

INSIDEAT

Steaming bowls of home-made pasta and crispy wood-fired pizzas – food is at the heart of Roman culture. Experience this heritage first-hand with a hands-on cooking class. Insideat offers immersive experiences led by local chefs, revealing the secrets behind traditional Italian dishes passed down through the generations. Discover the philosophy of *cucina casalinga* (home-style cooking), using fresh, local ingredients, and enjoy your creations with fellow food lovers. Hands-on classes range from a one-hour pizza-making workshop to a two-hour session on pasta, ravioli and tiramisù, all set in the warm environment of an authentic local restaurant. Roll fresh pasta by hand, perfect your pizza dough and master the essentials of Italian cooking! Classes are suitable for all levels. Contact us on WhatsApp chat +39 327 306 8995. Get 15% off with the code **ROUGHGUIDESROME** when booking online.

To help you order

waiters **cameriere** (man) / **cameriera** (woman)
Do you have a set menu? **Avete un menù a prezzo fisso?**
I'd like a/an/some... **Vorrei...**

beer **una birra**
bread **il pane**
butter **il burro**
coffee **un caffè**
fish **il pesce**
fruit **la frutta**
ice cream **un gelato**
meat **la carne**
milk **il latte**

pepper **il pepe**
potatoes **le patate**
salad **un'insalata**
salt **il sale**
soup **la minestra**
sugar **lo zucchero**
tea **un tè**
water **l'acqua**
wine **il vino**

Menu reader

aglio garlic
agnello lamb
albicocche apricots
aragosta lobster
arancia orange
bistecca beefsteak
braciola chop
calamari squid
carciofi artichokes
cozze mussels
crostacei shellfish
fegato liver
fiche figs
formaggio cheese
frutti di mare seafood
funghi mushrooms
lamponi raspberries
maiale pork

manzo beef
mela apple
melanzane aubergine
merluzzo cod
ostriche oysters
pesca peach
pollo chicken
pomodori tomatoes
prosciutto ham
rognoni kidneys
tacchino turkey
tonno tuna
trippa tripe
uovo egg
uva grapes
verdure vegetables
vitello veal
vongole clams

Places to eat

Each restaurant and café reviewed in this Guide is accompanied by a price category, based on the cost of a three-course meal (or similar) for two, including a bottle of house wine and service:

€€€€ = over €70
€€€ = €45–70
€€ = €25–45
€ = below €25

Colosseum

Luzzi Via di San Giovanni in Laterano 88, www.trattorialuzzi.it. A very popular neighbourhood *trattoria* a short walk away from the Colosseum. *Luzzi* is loud and cheerful and serves up good pizzas, pasta dishes and simple second courses of fish and meat. The outside tables operate all year round. Lunch and dinner. **€**

Piazza Navona and Pantheon

Da Baffetto Via del Governo Vecchio 114, 06-6861617. This pizzeria is a rowdy Roman institution, loved by all for the excellent thin, crispy-baked pizza that comes straight from its *forno a legna* (wood-fired oven). The simple cheese-blistered margherita is everyone's favourite; the chefs can't churn them out fast enough for the hungry crowd. No credit cards or reservations – just join the queue outside if there is one. Daily noon–1.30am. **€**

Casa Bleve Via del Teatro Valle 48–49, www.casableve.com. Real gastronomic experience of authentic Italian cuisine and excellent wine (one of Rome's oldest *enoteche*) served in the dining hall of a fifteenth-century palazzo; the cellars shelter remains of an ancient Roman wall. Gluten-free meals. Lunch and dinner. Closed Sun. **€€€**

Il Convivio Troiani Vicolo dei Soldati 31, www.ilconviviotroiani.com. One of Rome's top restaurants and with a Michelin star to prove it, run by the three amiable Troiani brothers, with Angelo helming the kitchen. Imaginative, un-Roman dishes such as quail leg stuffed with foie gras, or minced cuttlefish with roasted peppers. Excellent, fairly priced wine selection. Reservations recommended. Expect to pay about €70 or more per head. Dinner only; closed all day Sun. €€€€

Cul de Sac Piazza di Pasquino 73, www.enotecaculdesacroma.it. The oldest and one of the best-stocked wine bars in Rome. The space might be tight, but the atmosphere and prices are just right. The array of cheeses, cold meats, Middle Eastern-influenced snacks, hearty soups and salads is of consistently high quality. Be prepared to queue if you arrive at peak times. Lunch and dinner daily; open late. €€

Da Francesco Piazza del Fico 29, www.dafrancesco.it. A consistently popular and always buzzing *trattoria* serving traditional Roman and Italian fare at reasonable prices. The appetiser buffet is particularly rich, and it does crispy, wood-oven baked pizzas at dinner. Open daily for lunch and dinner. €€€

'Gusto Piazza Sant'Apollinare 41, www.gusto.it. From breakfast and brunch through lunch, *aperitivo* and dinner, *'Gusto* has a varied menu rooted in Italian tradition but drawing inspiration from modern and global culinary trends. The quality is always high, the raw ingredients are carefully selected, and service is fast. Elegant setting with a pleasant outdoor patio and a great wine cellar. Open daily. €€

Il Piccolo Via del Governo Vecchio 74, tel: 06-68801746. A lively and casual wine bar that offers a buffet serving a limited selection of traditional fare in a characterful neighbourhood. Warm dishes are only served at lunchtime; cold platters and salads are on offer in the evening. Eat here before heading to the Piazza Navona for a slice of street theatre. Open daily for lunch and dinner. €€

La Rosetta Via della Rosetta 8, www.larosetta.com. Considered to be the best seafood restaurant in Rome, *La Rosetta* plates up classic but creative plates along the likes of fillet of sea bass with red wine sauce and artichokes. Selection of international wines. Reservations essential. Daily noon–11pm; closed Mon. €€€€

Terra di Siena Piazza Pasquino 77/78, www.ristoranteterradisiena.com. A family-run haunt serving traditional dishes from the Tuscan hills. Carnivores will be spoiled for choice here, with a long list of meaty treats, and the 300-plus wine labels include all the Chiantis you can imagine. Open daily for lunch and dinner. €€

Campo de' Fiori and Ghetto

Buddy Corso Vittorio Emanuele II 107A, www.buddyroma.com. One of Rome's few vegetarian restaurants, *Buddy* is conveniently located just between Campo de' Fiori and Piazza Navona. The kitchen rustles up delicious veggie and vegan takes on classic Roman and Italian dishes such carbonara and lasagna *alla Bolognese*. There's also a buffet available every day until midday if you're in a hurry. Open daily from 10am; weekends from 9am. €€

Ditirambo Piazza della Cancelleria 74/75, www.ditiramboristorante.it. In this rustic and cosy space, tourists and locals alike feast on imaginative combinations such as ricotta flan served with sliced artichoke and a fruity pomegranate sauce. Also serves traditional well-cooked cuts of meat and fish dishes. The pasta is home-made, as are the mouth-watering sweets. Many options for vegetarians. Lunch and dinner. €€

Open Baladin Roma Via degli Specchi 6, www.baladin.it/open-baladin-roma. More than one hundred Italian artisanal beers and high-quality ingredients define this modern restaurant. Order a juicy steak or take your pick from the list of gourmet burgers, which includes the all-Italian buffalo mozzarella cheeseburger. Vegetarians can choose from a selection of salads and first courses. Friendly staff. Open daily for lunch and dinner. €€

Il Pagliaccio Via dei Banchi Vecchi 129a, www.ristoranteilpagliaccio.it. A highly innovative top-class gourmet experience is to be had in this refined two-Michelin-starred venue. Service is attentive and cordial, and there is an adventurous fixed tasting menu. A three-course lunch will set you back €85. Closed Sun and Mon; lunch only on Tues and Wed. €€€

Piperno Via Monte dei Cenci 9, www.ristorantepiperno.it. Opened in 1856, this long-time favourite in the heart of the Ghetto serves Roman-Jewish specialities, such as *carciofi alla giudia* (fried whole artichokes) and Jerusalem artichokes in a number of delicious variations, as well as fish, veal and pasta dishes. Reservations recommended. Dinner only; Sat lunch and dinner; Sun lunch only. Closed Mon. €€€

Al Pompiere Piazza delle Cinque Scole 28, www.alpompiereroma.com. Waistcoated waiters serve diners in the frescoed rooms of this first-floor restaurant located in the picturesque Palazzo Cenci. The dishes are Roman and Roman-Jewish and include many of the local staples such as *tonnarelli cacio e pepe* and excellent fried vegetables. The standard is consistently good. Lunch and dinner; closed Sun. €€€

Trattoria Moderna Vicolo dei Chiodaroli 16, tel: 06-68803423. *Trattoria Moderna* has an appealing modern decor of earthy tones. The owners are experienced Roman restaurateurs, and the menu is classic Mediterranean with a playful modern spin. Lunch and dinner daily. €€

Trattoria der Pallaro Largo del Pallaro 15, tel: 06-68801488. This quintessentially Roman *trattoria* is a reliable favourite for big appetites and smaller budgets. There is no menu, but for around €20 (house wine and water included) you'll be served several courses one after the other and will leave feeling satisfyingly full. The fare is not particularly sophisticated but is very tasty. The artichokes are excellent and the desserts home-made. The kitchen stays open until past midnight. No credit cards. Lunch and dinner daily. €

Piazza di Spagna and Tridente

Caffè Canova Atelier Canova Tadolini, Via del Babuino 150, www.canova tadolini.com. In 1818, renowned marble master Antonio Canova turned over his sculpture workshop to his favourite apprentice, Adamo Tadolini, and it remained in the family until 1967. Now it has been transformed into a museum-atelier and full-scale café and restaurant, where you can dine all day on small plates amid striking marble creations. Open daily til late. €€

Ristorante Dillà Via Mario de' Fiori 41, tel: 06-69797778. Roman-style tavern 200m from the Spanish Steps. Cosy interior furnished with recycled designer materials. Menu prepared by a passionate team of chefs and sommeliers, featuring exquisite appetisers and seafood. Open daily. €€

Nino Via Borgognona 11, www.ristorantenino.it. Good traditional Tuscan food and Chianti wine selections have been long frequented by the shop owners and patrons of this chic neighbourhood. *Nino* is reasonably priced for such an expensive area. Try the *taglioni con tartufo nero* (black truffle pasta). €€€

Obicà Mozzarella Bar Via dei Prefetti 26/a, www.obica.com. Touting itself as the first 'mozzarella bar' in Rome, this minimal chain restaurant pays homage to the delicious cheese that is delivered daily from the neighbouring Campania region. Customers can eat it sushi-style at counters or in a variety of dishes in the elegant restaurant. There are plenty of options for non-cheese eaters, scrumptious desserts and a very affordable lunch menu. Lunch and dinner daily. €€

Il Vero Alfredo Piazza Augusto Imperatore 30, www.ilveroalfredo.it. This historical restaurant run by third-generation noodle kings is an obligatory culinary stop for pasta lovers. It serves the famous 'Real Maestosissime' Fettuccine Alfredo Style. Douglas Fairbanks and Mary Pickford gifted a golden engraved spoon and fork to the first owner in tribute to his delicious and original meal. In addition to *fettuccine*, the place offers traditional Roman cuisine. Open for lunch and dinner; closed Mon. €€€

Via Veneto and Trevi Fountain

Doney Via Vittorio Veneto 125, www.restaurantdoney.com. Both the café and restaurant lounge attached to the historic *Excelsior Hotel* are *dolce vita* landmarks and warrant a visit. Constantly renovated and always achingly cool, *Doney* is the place for a cappuccino by day, an *aperitif* among the city's hip crowd, or a dinner of creative and sophisticated Italian cuisine. Open daily from 7am. €€€

Nanà Via della Panetteria 37, www.nanaviniecucina.it. Just a short walk from the Trevi Fountain, this restaurant is a real find in a generally overpriced and low-quality tourist area. The decor is chic and rustic, the staff friendly, and the food influenced by southern Italy, with excellent speciality dishes from the Calabria, Sicilia and Puglia regions. Lunch and dinner; closed Mon. €€

Pane e Salame Via di Santa Maria in Via 19, tel: 06-6791352. This small, cosy restaurant offers arguably the best sandwiches in Rome, together with excellent cold meat boards and paninis. Be prepared to wait as the place gets crowded. Open daily noon–10pm. €

Rinaldi al Quirinale Via Parma 11A, www.rinaldialquirinale.it. A charming restaurant, perfect for a romantic night out. Top dishes are sautéed mussels, oysters, rock lobster and pasta with porcini mushrooms. Friendly service and more than three hundred wine labels. Lunch and dinner daily. €€€

Trattoria Monti Via di S. Vito, 13/A, tel: 06-4466573. Very popular, family-run *trattoria* with friendly service and ambience. Excellent food from Le

Marche region and a decent wine list at reasonable prices. It gets very crowded, so book in advance. Vegetarian friendly. Lunch and dinner; Sun lunch only. Closed Mon. €

Vatican and Prati

L'Arcangelo Via G.G. Belli 59–61, www.larcangelo.com. The prints on the walls and linen tablecloths form an unexpected backdrop to some very imaginative culinary offerings and an understated gourmet experience. There's a reasonably priced taster menu of Roman cuisine. Lunch and dinner; closed Sun. €€

Osteria dell'Angelo Via G. Bettolo 24, tel: 06-3729470. This *trattoria* serves deliciously hearty Roman dishes at affordable prices. Truly a local experience, not known to most tourists. In the evening the restaurant serves a full menu for about €25. The staff may seem unfriendly at first, but it's part of the show. Mon–Sat lunch and dinner. €

Il Ristoro Via G. Palombini 27, tel: 06-6628666. A simple fish-focused bistro offering an intimate setting with only a few tables. The menu lists many different fish-based options, all extremely fresh, including an impressive raw seafood platter, spaghetti with bottarga (salted cured fish roe) and clams, *tonnarelli* with sea bass, fried calamari, tuna steak, and that day's catch, prepared in different ways. Carefully curated wine list with many great sparkling whites. €€€

Il Sorpasso Via Properzio 31/33, www.sorpasso.info. A ten-minute walk from St Peter's Square, *Il Sorpasso* is one of the hidden foodie gems of Rome. With dry meats hanging by the entrance, this non-touristy restaurant offers a wide range of menu items from classic pastas to grilled meats to fresh salads. Also a good place to stop for coffee, a glass of wine or a pastry after visiting the Vatican Museums. Open 7.30am–1am; Sat and Sun dinner only. €€

Trastevere and Testaccio

Ai Marmi Viale di Trastevere 53–59, tel: 06-5800919. Beloved by Romans and visitors alike, *Ai Marmi* is also known affectionately to Romans as *L'Obitorio* ('The Morgue'), because of its long marble tables on which patrons are seated close together in order to squeeze in as many as possible. The pizza, which you can see being made by expert *pizzaioli* in an open kitchen with a wood-fired oven, is some of the best in Rome. It gets very crowded, but this is a testament to the quality of the food; the atmosphere and sometimes haphazard service is all part of the experience. Be prepared to queue. Open 6.30am–2am; closed Wed. €

Antica Pesa Rome Via Garibaldi 18, www.anticapesa.it. Historical restaurant and wine cellar in the heart of Trastevere. Established in 1922, it offers an elegant fusion of the traditional and the modern, and its walls are frescoed by renewed artists. It is a recognised landmark for Roman dining, sometimes visited by celebrities. If the weather allows, you can enjoy meals in the beautiful terrace garden. Dinner only; closed Sun. €€€

Checchino dal 1887 Via di Monte Testaccio 30, www.checchino-dal-1887.com. An acclaimed first-rate *trattoria* serving traditional cuisine based on the cheap cuts and offal from Testaccio's slaughterhouse. Tripe, brains, liver, sweetbreads and intestines are loved by Romans, but there's much more on offer to keep less adventurous palates happy. Lunch and dinner. Closed Mon and Tues. Reserve for dinner. €€€

Glass Hostaria Vicolo del Cinque 58, www.glasshostaria.it. Excellent taster menus, home-made bread and creative dishes such as *tagliolini al nero di seppia con capesante, zucchine e pomodorini* (black squid-ink pasta with scallops, courgettes and small tomatoes) and *tortelli verdi di trota e ortica con pomodoro fresco* (trout and nettle *tortelli* served with fresh tomato), make this restaurant in Trastevere a memorable experience. Dinner only. Closed Mon and Tues. €€€€

Trapizzino Piazza Trilussa 46, www.trapizzino.it. With four locations in Trastevere, Testaccio, Ponte Milvio and Mercato Centrale Rome in Termini station, *Trapizzino* is not to be missed. From the words '*tramezzino*', a filled, usually triangular Italian sandwich, and '*pizza*', a *trapizzino* is a pizza pocket with a roster of tasty fillings including hunter's chicken, cow tongue in green sauce and aubergine bake. The *supplì* – breaded and deep-fried balls of risotto with a melted cheesy centre – are out of this world. Open until 1 or 2am. €

Trimani Wine Bar Via Cernaia 37b, www.trimani.com. An excellent choice of wines (the Trimani family first became famous for their nearby wine store) and good food served in an elegant and friendly atmosphere. Sample a number of wines by the glass, accompanied by a light or full meal at reasonable prices. Warm and welcoming service. Open all day; closed Sun. €€

Further afield in Rome

La Pergola at the Rome Cavalieri Via Cadlolo 101, www.romecavalieri.com. This elegant penthouse restaurant with three Michelin stars has a spectacular view overlooking the city and Roman hills, and an acclaimed chef who creates superb Mediterranean dishes. Reservations essential. Dinner only. Closed Sun and Mon. €€€€

Romeow Cat Bistrot Via Francesco Negri 15, www.romeowcatbistrot.com. A vegan restaurant that changes its menu with the seasons to use the freshest ingredients. Meat-eaters and -avoiders alike will be bowled over by the quality of food at *Romeow*. The care taken by the chefs over each dish is palpable, and their desserts are famous; there's also a tasting menu for those who can't decide. Happy cats weave between tables and across a maze of planks high above the dining tables while you eat. With warm service and wonderfully friendly staff, *Romeow* is well worth the venture out of the centre. Closed Mondays. €€€

Travel essentials

Practical information

Accessible travel	**127**
Accommodation	**127**
Airports	**128**
Apps	**128**
Bicycles and scooters	**129**
Budgeting for your trip	**129**
Camping	**129**
Climate	**130**
Crime and safety	**130**
Driving	**130**
Electricity	**131**
Embassies and consulates	**132**
Emergencies	**132**
Getting there	**132**
Guides and tours	**133**
Health and medical care	**133**
Language	**134**
LGBTQ+ travellers	**134**
Money	**135**
Opening hours	**135**
Police	**136**
Public holidays	**136**
Religion	**137**
Telephones	**137**
Time zones	**138**
Tipping	**138**
Toilets	**138**
Tourist information	**138**
Transport	**139**
Visas and entry requirements	**141**
Websites	**141**

Accessible travel

It has to be said that Rome is not a particularly accessible city; cobbled streets and steep hills are just two of the problems facing travellers with disabilities. St Peter's, the Vatican Museums, Castel Sant'Angelo, Galleria Doria Pamphili, San Giovanni in Laterano, Galleria Borghese, Galleria Nazionale d'Arte Moderna and a few other, more minor museums are wheelchair-accessible. Up-to-date information on access to sights, monuments and hotels is available from Roma Per Tutti (Mon–Fri 9am–5pm; tel: 06-57177094, www.romapertutti.it).

Accommodation

Rome's array of lodgings ranges from the spartan to the palatial. Hotels (*alberghi*) are classified in five categories and graded from one to five stars, based on the amenities and comfort they offer. The Italian National Tourist Board no longer uses the term *pensione* in its classifications; these family-style boarding houses are now graded as hotels, usually one or two stars. Some religious institutions also take guests at reasonable rates.

High season is considered to be Christmas, New Year and Easter to October (though it may be advisable to avoid the hot and humid months of July and August). At these times booking ahead is important. For the rest of the year, you can normally find accommodation in your preferred category without difficulty, though decent inexpensive hotels are usually snapped up far ahead. Rome's official tourist office operates an information website (www.060608.it), an information line (tel: 06-0608) and information kiosks (*punti informativi turistici* or PIT) in various locations around the city (see page 141). All provide up-to-date hotel listings and may be able to help with your booking. Family-run B&Bs can be found at www.bed-and-breakfast.it, while www.airbnb.com lists a wide selection of private apartments available for short-term rent.

Room rates should include service and taxes. By law, hotels have to charge an additional tourist tax of €4–10 per person, per night. Most hotels have air-conditioning; in lower-category hotels it may cost extra.

At Fiumicino, the *Hilton Rome Airport* hotel is near the main terminal (tel: 06-65258).

> I'd like a single/double room with bath/shower. **Vorrei una camera singola/doppia con bagno/doccia**
> What's the rate per night? **Qual è il prezzo per notte?**

Airports

Rome is served by two airports, Leonardo da Vinci, more commonly referred to as **Fiumicino** (FCO), 30km (18 miles) southwest of the city, and **Ciampino** (CIA), 15km (9 miles) southeast of the city on the Via Appia Nuova (for information on both airports visit www.adr.it). Fiumicino handles mainly scheduled air traffic; most charter companies and low-cost airlines use Ciampino.

Fiumicino is connected by train to Termini railway station (about every 15–30min; journey 30min; daily 6.23am–11.23pm, from Rome 5.35am–10.35pm); €14; guaranteed on strike days), and to Trastevere railway station (every 15min, on weekends and holidays and after 9pm every 30min; journey 31 minutes; first and last departures 5.57am and 11.27pm; €8). A taxi from Fiumicino to the city centre costs €55; €40 from Ciampino. These fixed fares, set by the authorities, are valid for up to four people with luggage at any time of day or night. A late-night Cotral bus runs between Fiumicino and the Tiburtina and Termini train stations when there is no train service. Termini is connected to metro lines A and B, and to buses that go all over the city; Trastevere is linked to the city centre by tram #8.

There's also the Terravision coach service between Termini train station and Fiumicino and Ciampino airports; tickets cost €6.50 and can be bought online at www.terravision.eu, at the airports' Terravision kiosk or at Termini station's Via Marsala entrance (in front of *Terracaffè*). Termini station has luggage storage facilities.

Apps

For taxis, download the Italy-wide taxi app **itTaxi**. **Uber** in Rome works in collaboration with local taxi companies. The app **Moovit** gives real-time information on bus transport and schedules. **Waidy – App per bere** guides users to the closest public drinking fountain *(nasone)*.

Bicycles and scooters

There are plenty of bike-rental companies in Rome, including Topbike Rental (Via Labicana 49; www.topbikerental.com), offering all types of bikes. The best day to cycle in the city is Sunday, when several roads are closed to cars.

For faster and more authentic wheels, check out Bici e Baci scooter rentals (Via del Viminale and Via Cavour 302; www.bicibaci.com). Wearing a helmet is compulsory at all times.

Budgeting for your trip

Buses, metro and trains (urban network). Standard fare (*biglietto* or BIT) €1.50 (valid for 1hr 40min); one-day ticket (ROMA 24H or *biglietto integrato giornaliero*) €7; two- and three-day tickets (ROMA 48H and ROMA 72H) €12.50 and €18, respectively; weekly ticket (CIS or *carta integrata settimanale*) €24, which allows unlimited travel on all trams, local trains, Cotral buses and the metro for seven days. For timetables, fares and maps, see www.atac.roma.it.

Entertainment. Cinema tickets €8.50–12, nightclub (entry and first drink) €15–25, outdoor opera €20–120.

Hotels. For a double room with bath, including tax and service, prices range from €60 for a one-star hotel (cheaper if it has dorm beds) near the station to over €1200 for a suite in a five-star near the Spanish Steps. Almost all hotels lower their prices in the low season.

Meals and drinks. Continental breakfast €10, lunch/dinner in a fairly good establishment €20–50, coffee served at a table €2–5, served at the bar €0.80–1.20. Also at the bar: bottle of beer €2–5, soft drinks €2–4, aperitif €3 and up.

Museums. Tickets €12–21, and most museums offer free entry once a month (usually on the first Sunday).

Camping

Rome and its environs have some twenty official campsites, most equipped with electricity, water and toilets. They are listed on the website www.camping.it. You can also ask in any tourist information point (see page 141) for a full list of sites and rates. A popular campsite is *Flaminio Village* (www.villageflaminio.com), just 6km (4 miles) north of the city centre.

Climate

From June to mid-September, temperatures in Rome range from warm to sizzling. It is not unusual to find temperatures above 35°C (95°F) in the afternoon in July and August, when it is best to keep major sightseeing to the morning and late afternoon and stay out of the fierce sun during the hottest parts of the day. Winters are cool, often cold, and at times rainy, with occasional snow, but there are many sunny days. Spring and autumn are mild, and the best time to visit.

Crime and safety (see also Emergencies)

Pickpockets and purse-snatchers are not uncommon in Rome and tourists are a favourite target. Be careful on crowded public transport (beware the tourist-filled buses #64 and #40 from Termini station to the Vatican, and the metro). Groups of begging children are adept pickpockets, lingering around Termini, the Forum, Largo di Torre Argentina and crowded shopping streets.

It is a good idea to make photocopies of your airline tickets, driving licence, passport and other vital documents to facilitate reporting any theft and obtaining replacements. Report thefts to the police, so that you have a statement to file with your insurance claim. The central police station is at Questura Centrale, Via San Vitale 15, tel: 06-46861. For emergencies, call 113.

> I want to report a theft. **Voglio denunciare un furto.**
> My wallet/handbag/passport/ticket has been stolen. **Mi hanno rubato il portafoglio/la borsa/il passaporto/il biglietto.**

Driving

Driving in the city is not advisable, not least because much of the historic centre consists of traffic-restricted zones or pedestrian-only zones, and parking is difficult at best. It is easiest to explore the city on foot or by metro, saving the car for excursions outside the centre.

If you need help. Emergency telephone boxes are located at regular intervals on the *autostrade* in case of breakdowns or other difficulties. The **ACI** (Automobile Club of Italy; www.aci.it) runs an efficient breakdown service. If you dial **803116**, you can access its English-speaking operators 24hr a day.

Driving in Rome. If you must drive in Rome, make sure you check to the right and left and your rear-view mirror all the time, and don't take priority for granted with green lights and pedestrian crossings. To progress in a traffic jam, inch gently but confidently forward. Be careful of scooters suddenly passing you on either side.

> I've had a breakdown. **Ho avuto un guasto.**
> There's been an accident. **C'è stato un incidente.**

In the city centre between the river, Piazza del Popolo, Piazza di Spagna, Santa Maria Maggiore and the Colosseum, as well as at night in the San Lorenzo district and across the river in Trastevere, a traffic-restricted *zona a traffico limitato* (ZTL) operates Mon–Sat day and night, times vary (for details visit www.060608.it). If in doubt, read the electronic signs at the access of the Limited Traffic Zone: '*varco attivo*' means that access is restricted, '*varco non attivo*' means no restrictions. Exceptions to this rule are taxis, buses and cars with permits.

Fuel. Fuel *(benzina)* comes unleaded *(senza piombo or verde)* or as diesel *(gasolio)*. Liquid propane gas is marked gpl.

Parking. Parking is one of Rome's greatest challenges. Blue lines designate paid parking areas. Buy a ticket from one of the coin meters. In the centre of Rome the largest and most accessible car parks are: Roma Garage San Pietro at Piazza di Santa Maria alle Fornaci 26 (www.parkimeter.com), open 24hr; Parking Lago Eur (www.apcoa.it) on Piazza Terracini, open 24hr; or (the largest, always open) at Villa Borghese (www.sabait.it), entrance at Viale del Galoppatoio 33.

Electricity

Electric current is 220 volts, 50 Hz ac. Bring a multiple adapter plug *(un adattatore)*, or buy one as required.

Embassies and consulates

AUS Via Antonio Bosio 5; tel: 06-852721, www.italy.embassy.gov.au
Canada Via Zara 30; tel: 06-854441, www.international.gc.ca/country-pays/italy-italie/
Ireland Villa Spada, Via Giacomo Medici 1; tel: 06-5852381, www.dfa.ie/irish-embassy/italy
NZ Via Clitunno 44; tel: 06-8537501, www.mfat.govt.nz
South Africa Via Tanaro 14; tel: 06-852541, http://lnx.sudafrica.it
UK Via XX Settembre 80a; tel: 06-42200001, www.gov.uk/government/world/italy
US Via Vittorio Veneto 121; tel: 06-46741, https://it.usembassy.gov

Emergencies

General emergency number (for all services) **112**; State police **113**; Ambulance **118**; Fire **115**; Road assistance (ACI) **803116**.

> Careful! **Attenzione!**
> Help! **Aiuto!**
> Stop thief! **Al ladro!**

Getting there (see also Airports)

By air. Rome's Fiumicino (Leonardo da Vinci) Airport is linked by frequent direct service to cities in Europe, North America, the Middle East and Africa. Average flying times are: New York–Rome 8hr; Los Angeles–Rome 13hr; London–Rome 2hr 30min; Sydney–Rome 26hr.

By car. The Channel Tunnel and Cross-Channel car ferries link the UK with France, Belgium and Holland. Once on the Continent, you can put your car on a train to Milan (starting points include Boulogne, Paris and Cologne). Alternatively, you can drive from the Channel coast to Rome without leaving a motorway. The main north–south (Milan–Florence–Reggio di Calabria) and east–west (L'Aquila–Civitavecchia) motorways connect with Rome via a huge ring motorway *(grande raccordo anulare)*.

By rail. Interrail cards are valid in Italy, as is the Eurail pass for non-European residents (purchase it before you leave home). You can find out more details at www.interrail.eu and www.eurail.com. To buy Interrail passes in the UK, visit www.sncf-connect.com.

Guides and tours

Many private firms offer guided bus tours. An English-speaking travel operation located near the station, **Enjoy Rome** (Via Vespasiano 46 B 8; tel: 06-4450735, www.enjoyrome.com) offers inexpensive walking tours of Rome daily. Several companies offer tours in the open-topped double-decker buses that usually start at Termini station and loop past the city's main monuments. Tour operators include **City Sightseeing Roma** (www.city-sightseeing.it), **Big Bus Roma** (www.bigbustours.com) and **Grayline** (http://graylinerome.com); 48hr tickets start from about €37 (slightly less in low season). The whole tour usually lasts around two hours and the buses operate between 9am and 5pm. You can hop off and on at any of 8–10 stops on the route.

Health and medical care

EU residents are entitled to the same treatment as Italian citizens (that is to say, emergency medical and hospital treatment) but should obtain the European Health Insurance Card. In the UK, the EHIC card has been replaced by the GHIC (Global Health Insurance Card). If you still have an EHIC, you can continue to use it until the expiry date on the card, at which point you should apply for a GHIC; visit www.nhs.uk. To cover all eventualities, travel insurance is recommended. Non-EU visitors should always have private medical insurance.

Rome's tap water is not only safe for drinking, but is also considered the best in Italy. Bring an empty bottle when you're out and about, and fill it up at one of the ever-running street fountains.

Pharmacies. The Italian *farmacia* is normally open Mon–Fri 9.30am–1pm and 3.30–7.30/8pm, plus Saturday mornings. Usually one operates out of hours in each district on a rotating basis. Its address will be posted in the windows of all pharmacies in the area. Some are open 24hr, like the Farmacia Internazionale (Piazza Barberini 49; tel: 06-4871195).

> I need a doctor/a dentist. **Ho bisogno di un medico/dentista.**
> Where's the nearest (all-night) chemist? **Dov'è la farmacia (di turno) più vicina?**

Language

You will not find English spoken everywhere in Rome, as you do in some other European cities. However, Italians are usually helpful and quick to understand what you want. Italians appreciate foreigners making an effort to speak their language, even if it's only a few words. In the major hotels and shops, staff usually speak some English.

Bear in mind the following tips on pronunciation:

'c' is pronounced like 'ch' in change when followed by 'e' or 'i'.
'ch' together sounds like the 'c' in cat.
'g' followed by an 'e' or an 'i' is pronounced like 'j' in jet.
'gh' together sounds like the 'g' in gap.
'gl' together sounds like the 'lli' in million.
'gn' is pronounced like 'ni' in onion.
'sc' + 'i' is pronounced like 'she'.

LGBTQ+ travellers

Rome can be less open-minded when it comes to the LGBTQ+ community than most other major cities in Western Europe. Openly gay couples are not the norm here, but they are generally tolerated and respected. There are more and more gay and gay-friendly clubs and events, including the Pride parade in June, and many events hosted by GIAM (www.facebook.com/GIAMRoma, www.gayrome4u.com, www.travelgay.com/destination/gay-italy/gay-rome). The city's LGBTQ+ area is concentrated in and around a bar called *Coming Out* (www.comingout.it), on Via di San Giovanni in Laterano 8, close to the Colosseum. Associations like Mario Mieli (Via Efeso 2A;

tel: 06-5413985, www.mariomieli.org) and ARCIGay (Via Zabaglia 14; tel: 06-64501102, www.arcigayroma.it) provide information.

Money

Currency. Italy's monetary unit is the euro (€), which is divided into 100 cents. Banknotes are available in denominations of €500, €200, €100, €50, €20, €10 and €5. There are coins of €2 and €1, and of 50, 20, 10, 5, 2 and 1 cent.

Currency exchange. Currency exchange offices *(cambio)* in the touristy areas are usually open daily 8.30am–7.30pm; some may close on Sunday. Both *cambio* and banks charge a commission. Banks generally offer higher exchange rates and lower commissions. Passports are sometimes required when changing money.

> I want to change some pounds/dollars. **Vorrei cambiare delle sterline/dei dollari.**
> Can I pay with a credit card? **Posso pagare con la carta di credito?**

Opening hours

Most offices, larger stores and shops in the *centro storico* operate non-stop all day. But much of the city shuts or slows down after lunch.

Shops. Mon–Sat 9am–1pm and 4–8pm (winter 3.30–7.30pm). Half-day closing is usually Monday morning. However, most shops in the centre (Via del Corso, Via Nazionale, Via del Tritone) are open 10am–8pm, and department stores are also open all day. Food stores are open 8.30am–1.30pm and 4–7.30pm (summer until 8pm). Except for supermarkets, there is a half-day closing, usually Thursday afternoon in winter, and Saturday afternoon in summer. Most shops in the city centre or in commercial districts, including supermarkets, now stay open through lunch and on Sunday. Smaller shops and boutiques usually close for at least two weeks between July and mid-September.

Banks. Mon–Fri 8.30am–1.30pm, and again for two hours or so in the afternoon (usually 2.40–4.30pm).

Pharmacies. 8.30am–1pm and 4–8pm (some 24hr, see page 133).

Churches. Open daily from early morning to noon or 12.30pm, and 4 or 5–7pm. They discourage Sunday morning visits except for those attending Mass. Larger churches and basilicas are open all day.

Museums and historic sites. These are usually open Tues–Sun 9am–7pm (sometimes earlier), but hours vary.

Police

The municipal police *(vigili urbani)*, dressed in navy blue or summer white uniforms with white helmets, handle city traffic and other city police tasks. Interpreters display a special badge, which indicates the languages they speak.

The *carabinieri*, in dark blue uniforms with a red stripe down their trousers, deal with serious crimes, demonstrations and military affairs. The national, or state, police *(polizia di stato)*, distinguished by their navy-blue jackets and light-blue trousers, handle other police and administrative matters (See also Driving.). In case of an emergency or if you need to report a theft or a lost document, both *polizia* and *carabinieri* will be able to help. The emergency number, tel: 113, will get you police assistance.

> Where's the nearest police station? **Dov'è il posto di polizia più vicino?**

Public holidays

Banks, government offices and most shops and museums close on public holidays. When a major holiday falls on a Thursday or a Tuesday, many Italians may make a *ponte* (bridge) to the weekend, meaning that Friday or Monday is taken, too. The most important holidays are:

1 January *Capodanno* New Year's Day
6 January *Epifania* Epiphany
25 April *Festa della Liberazione* Liberation Day

1 May *Primo Maggio* May Day
2 June *Festa della Repubblica* Republic Day
15 August *Ferragosto* Feast of the Assumption
1 November *Ognissanti* All Saints' Day
8 December *Immacolata Concezione* Immaculate Conception
25 December *Natale* Christmas Day
26 December *Santo Stefano* Boxing Day
Moveable date *Pasquetta* Easter Monday

In addition, Rome has a local holiday on 29 June, the *Festa di San Pietro e San Paolo*, the Feast of St Peter and St Paul, the city's patron saints, when many offices and shops are closed. If you're hoping to see the Pope's Mass, which is usually held at 10am, aim to arrive early at St Peter's Square, as there are massive crowds. It's worth it for the beautiful visuals, though; St Peter's Square is traditionally decorated with flowers and petals.

Religion

All places of worship require modest clothing, meaning no bare shoulders or legs. It is always a good idea to have a scarf or sarong handy, in case of last-minute church visits.

Telephones

Most phone booths around town have been dismantled and public pay phones can now only be found in train stations, airports and schools. Only some accept coins, and others require phone cards *(scheda telefonica)*, which cost from €2.50 upwards. Credit-card phones charge very high fees.

Since phone services are expensive in Italy, it may be a good idea to buy an international phone card while staying in Rome. Sold at most newsagents, these cards allow you to call abroad at very low cost using a freephone number.

Those staying for longer periods of time may want to look into getting an Italian SIM for their mobile. Please note, your passport or European ID card will be required for registration, so take either with you. The main phone companies (Tim, Vodafone, Wind, Poste Mobile and Tre) constantly change their tariffs, so it's best to compare prices before choosing one. For Italian directory enquiries, call tel: 1254 or tel: 1240; international enquiries, tel: 892 412, national and international calls via 24hr operator, tel: 170. Direct dialling for Australia tel: 0061; Canada tel: 001; Ireland tel: 00353; South Africa tel: 0027; UK tel: 0044; US tel: 001.

Time zones

Italy follows Central European Time (GMT + 1). As in the UK, from the last Sunday in March to the last Sunday in October, clocks are put ahead one hour (GMT + 2). The following is a chart of summer times:

New York	London	**Italy**	Jo'burg	Sydney	Auckland
6am	11am	**noon**	noon	8pm	10pm

Tipping

Though a service charge is added to most restaurant bills *(servizio incluso)*, it is customary to leave an additional nominal tip, from a couple of euros up to ten percent of the bill. It is also usual to give porters, door staff, garage attendants and others a little something for their services. As a rough guide, give a hotel porter €1.50 per bag, a lavatory attendant €0.50. Tip tour guides up to five percent. Tipping taxi drivers is optional; €2 will suffice.

Toilets

Sometimes toilets will be labelled in Italian: *Uomini* is for men, *Donne* for women; *Signori* with a final 'i' is for men, but *Signore* with a final 'e' means women. Some facilities are unisex.

Tourist information

The **Italian National Tourist Board** (*Ente Nazionale Italiano per il Turismo*, abbreviated ENIT; www.italia.it) is represented in Italy and abroad. It publishes detailed brochures with up-to-date information on accommodation, transport, general tips and useful addresses for tourists.

The Tourist Board in Rome operates an information line (Mon–Sun 9am–9pm; tel: 060608) in six languages and a website (www.060608.it) that also lists current exhibitions, concerts and events. Visit www.turismoroma.it for further information.

There are also several tourist information points maintained by the city council dotted across the streets and open daily from 9.30am–6.30pm. These are at Castel Sant'Angelo–Piazza Pia; Fori Imperiali–Piazza del Tempio della Pace; Piazza delle Cinque Lune (Piazza Navona); Via Giolitti (Stazione Termini); Via dell'Olmata (Santa Maria Maggiore); Via Nazionale (Palazzo delle Esposizioni); Via Minghetti (Fontana di Trevi); and Ciampino and Fiumicino airports.

> Where's the nearest tourist office? **Dov'è l'ufficio turistico più vicino?**

Transport

Metropolitana. Rome has two main underground railway routes, Line A and Line B. Line A runs from Battistini in the west of the city southeast to Anagnina, stopping at more than twenty stations and passing close to many popular tourist sights (including the Vatican Museums and the Spanish Steps). Line B runs from Rebibbia in the northeastern part of the city through Stazione Termini to Laurentina (passing by the Colosseum and the suburb of EUR) in the southwest. The two lines intersect only once, at Stazione Termini. Local trains to Ostia Antica and Lido di Ostia (Rome's closest beach) leave from the station adjacent to the Piramide metro stop (Line B). A third line, C, runs from Monte Compatri-Pantano in the eastern suburbs to San Giovanni near the city centre, where it meets Line A. The metro runs 5.30am–11.30pm (Sat until 12.30am), though is liable to close earlier for long stretches of time when work is being done on the line; always check the time of the last train.

Metro stations are identified by a large red sign emblazoned with a white letter 'M'. Tickets are sold at newsstands, tobacconists and machines at the metro stations.

Buses and trams. Rome's red, silver and orange buses serve every corner of the city. Although crowded on certain routes and at rush hours, they are an inexpensive way of getting around. Each bus stop *(fermata)* indicates the buses stopping there, their routes and frequency. Tickets must be bought in advance from ATAC booths, some newsstands and tobacconists, or automatic dispensers. It is also possible to charge the ticket directly to your credit or debit card once you board the bus. Only one card per person is allowed, so if you are travelling with others, each person will need to have their own card. If you switch to another bus, remember to tap your card again: you will only be charged once. There are vending machines on most of the trams. Enter the bus by the rear or front doors and punch your ticket in the machine; exit by the middle doors; remember that you must ring the bell before your stop. The current system is steadily being overhauled, with more ecological and efficient buses replacing the old ones. Trams are mainly used by commuters and connect the city centre with suburbs such as Porta Maggiore or Ostia Antica. Note that ATAC tickets and passes entitle the holder to free travel on urban tram routes only. For visitors, the most useful lines are #2 to Piazza del Popolo, Villa Borghese, the Modern Art Gallery and the Olympic Stadium, and #3, which passes by Circus Maximus, the Colosseum and St John Lateran.

Tickets. A single ticket is valid for 1hr 40min and can be used on as many buses as you wish, but can be used only once on the metro or train. A 24hr ticket (BIG) lets you travel as much as you like by train, bus and metro. Weekly tickets (CIS) are sold at the ATAC (transport authority) information booth in Piazza dei Cinquecento, in front of Stazione Termini.

> Where's the nearest bus stop/ underground (subway) station? **Dov'è la fermata d'autobus/la stazione della metropolitana più vicina?**
> When's the next bus/train to…? **Quando parte il prossimo autobus/treno per…?**
> I'd like a ticket to... **Vorrei un biglietto per…**

> single (one-way) **andata**
> return (round trip) **andata e ritorno**

Taxis. Rome's licensed white taxis (*tassì* or *taxi*) can be flagged, but it is easier to find them at taxi ranks (in the historic centre two useful ones are located at Largo di Torre Argentina and Piazza Venezia, on the western side of Piazza Madonna di Loreto), or summon them by telephone (tel: 06-6645 or 06-3570). The rates are posted inside.

The meter starts at €3 (€5 10pm–6am), and €1.14–1.70 is charged for each kilometre, depending how fast the car is proceeding. There is a surcharge for holidays, Sundays and luggage (the first piece is free, each additional piece costs €1). The law-fixed fare for the journey from/to Fiumicino airport to/from inside the city walls is €55 for up to four people including luggage; €40 to/from Ciampino. Tariffs outside the *gra* (Rome's major ring road) are much higher. Tips are optional. Beware of the non-metered unlicensed taxis (*abusivi*), which are often found at the airport and railway stations.

Visas and entry requirements

For citizens of the EU, a valid passport or identity card is all that is needed to enter Italy for up to ninety days within any 180-day period. Citizens of Australia, Canada, New Zealand, the UK and the US require only a valid passport.

For stays of more than ninety days in a 180-day period a visa or residence permit is required.

Websites

A number of websites provide helpful information for tourists:
www.060608.it The city council's official tourist information site, featuring concert, event and exhibition listings, museum hours and lists of hotels and restaurants.
www.museiincomune.it Handy museum details.
www.enjoyrome.com Useful English-language site.
www.atac.roma.it Public transport.
www.turismoroma.it Official tourist site with essential information for visitors.

Index

A
Apostolic Library 79
Appian Way 90
aqueducts 92
Ara Pacis Augustae 61
Arch of Constantine 47
Arch of Septimius Severus 42
Arch of Titus 44
Area Sacra Argentina 53
Aventine Hill 83

B
Baths of Caracalla 47
Bernini, Lorenzo 50, 65
Bocca della Verita 57
Boncompagni Ludovisi collection 51
Borgia Apartments 79
Borromini 65, 88
Bramante 84

C
Caffè Greco 58
Campo de' Fiori 54
Capitoline Hill 36
Castel Sant'Angelo 71
catacombs 91
Cavalieri di Malta 84
Centrale Montemartini 92
Cerveteri 97
Chapel of Nicholas V 79
children 105
cinema 100
Circus Maximus 45
Circus of Maxentius 92
classical music 99
Colosseum 38, 45
Column of Phocas 42
Crypta Balbi 54
culture 99
Curia 40

D
Diocletian's Baths 86
Domine Quo Vadis 90
Domus Augustana 45
Domus Aurea 45
Domus Flavia 45

E
eating out 114
Esquilino 85
Etruscan Museum 68
Etruscan necropolis 97
EUR 94

F
festivals and events 106
Fontana della Barcaccia 58
Fontana delle Api 65
Fontana delle Tartarughe 56
Fontana del Tritone 65
Fosse Ardeatine 91
Fountain of the Four Rivers 51

G
Galleria Borghese 67
Galleria Nazionale d'Arte Antica 65
Galleria Nazionale d'Arte Moderna e Contemporanea 68
Gallery of Pius IV 73
Gesu, Il 53

Gianicolo 83

H
House of Augustus 44
House of Livia 44
House of the Vestal Virgins 43

I
Imperial Fora 38

J
Jewish Ghetto 56

K
Keats-Shelley Museum 58

L
Lapis Niger 41
Lido di Ostia 97

M
MACRO 68
markets 103
MAXXI 68
Michelangelo 75, 80
Monti 85
Musei Capitolini 36
Museo Barracco 55
Museo Carlo Bilotti 68
Museo di Roma in Trastevere 83
Museo Etrusco 77
Museo Pio Clementino 77
music venues 100

N
necropolis 76

INDEX

nightlife 100
  bars 101
  clubs 100

O
obelisk 87
opera and ballet 99
Ostia Antica 96
Ostiense 92

P
Palace of Domitian 45
Palatine Hill 44
Palazzo Altemps 51
Palazzo Barberini 65
Palazzo dei Conservatori 36
Palazzo del Quirinale 63
Palazzo Doria Pamphili 52
Palazzo Farnese 54
Palazzo Massimo 86
Palazzo Montecitorio 60
Palazzo Nuovo 36
Palazzo Senatorio 35
Palazzo Spada 54
Palazzo Venezia 34
Pantheon 48
Papal Apartments 72
Piazza Colonna 59
Piazza del Campidoglio 34
Piazza del Popolo 60
Piazza di Spagna 57
Piazza Garibaldi 83
Piazza Navona 50
Piazza Pia 73
Piazza Venezia 33
Pieta, the 75
Pinacoteca Capitolina 36
Pinacoteca Vaticana 81
Pincio Gardens 61
Ponte Sant'Angelo 71
Pope Francis 75
Porta del Popolo 60
Protestant Cemetery 84

R
Raphael Rooms 78
Roman Forum 39
Rostra 42

S
Sala Marco Aurelio 35
San Carlo alle Quattro Fontane 64
San Clemente 89
Sancta Sanctorum 89
San Giovanni in Laterano 88
San Paolo Fuori le Mura 93
San Pietro in Vincoli 87
Santa Cecilia in Trastevere 82
Santa Maria della Vittoria 66
Santa Maria del Popolo 60
Santa Maria in Aracoeli 37
Santa Maria in Cosmedin 56
Santa Maria in Trastevere 82
Santa Maria Maggiore 87
Sant'Andrea al Quirinale 64
Santa Sabina 84
Sant'Ignazio 52
Scala Santa 88
shopping 102
  antiques 103
  fashion 103
  markets 103
Sistine Chapel 79
Spanish Steps 58
sports 105
  basketball 105
  football 105
  rugby 105
St Peter's Basilica 73
St Peter's Square 74
Synagogue 57

T
Tempio di Rotondo 57
Temple of Antoninus and Faustina 43
Temple of Castor and Pollux 43
Temple of Julius Caesar 43
Temple of Saturn 42
Temple of Vesta 43
Testaccio 84
Theatre of Marcellus 56
Tiber Island 81
Tiempetto 83
Tivoli 93
Tomb of Cecilia Metella 92
Trajan's Column 38
Trajan's Forum Museum 39
Trajan's Markets 38
Trastevere 82
Trevi Fountain 62
Tridente 59
Trinita dei Monti 58

V
Vatican Museums 76
Vatican, the 69
Via Appia Antica 90
Via dei Pastini 52
Via del Corso 59
Via Veneto 66
Villa Adriana 94
Villa Borghese park 66
Villa dei Quintili 92
Villa d'Este 94
Villa Gregoriana 95
Villa Medici 61
Vittoriano 33

THE MINI ROUGH GUIDE TO
ROME

Second Edition 2025

Editor: Joanna Reeves
Original author: Patricia Schultz
Updater: Solveig Steinhardt
Picture Editor: Piotr Kala
Picture Manager: Tom Smyth
Cartography update: Katie Bennett
Layout: Grzegorz Madejak
Production Operations Manager: Katie Bennett
Publishing Technology Manager: Rebeka Davies
Head of Publishing: Sarah Clark
Photography credits: All images **Shutterstock** except: Britta Jaschinski/Apa Publications 102; Fotolia 88; iStock 24; Leonardo 14BR; Ming Tang-Evans/Apa Publications 21, 37, 45, 51, 63, 65, 69, 70, 72, 74, 77, 82, 86, 92
Cover credits: Spanish Steps **Pajor Pawel/Shutterstock**

About the author
Solveig Steinhardt is a travel writer, journalist and editor who lives between Tuscany, where she grew up, and Berlin. Her work has appeared in many travel outlets, including BBC Travel, Michelin Guides, and the *Toronto Star*, and she is the former editor of travel magazines *Where Rome* and *Where Berlin*. Solveig loves to spend her time exploring the unbeaten paths of Southern Europe and is particularly passionate about the urban and natural histories of coastal areas, architectural details, lost dialects and local culinary traditions.

Distribution
UK, Ireland and Europe: Apa Publications (UK) Ltd; mail@roughguides.com
United States and Canada: Two Rivers; ips@ingramcontent.com
Australia and New Zealand: Woodslane; info@woodslane.com.au
Worldwide: Apa Publications (UK) Ltd; mail@roughguides.com

Special Sales, Content Licensing and CoPublishing
Rough Guides can be purchased in bulk quantities at discounted prices. We can create special editions, personalized jackets and corporate imprints tailored to your needs.
mail@roughguides.com

roughguides.com

EU Representative
LOGOS EUROPE, 9 rue Nicolas Poussin, 17000, LA ROCHELLE, France; Contact@logoseurope.eu; +33 (0) 667937378

Printed by Finidr in Czech Republic

ISBN: 9781835292211

This book was produced using **Typefi** automated publishing software.

A catalogue record for this book is available from the British Library

All Rights Reserved
© 2025 Apa Digital AG
License edition © Apa Publications Ltd UK

No part of this book may be reproduced, stored in a retrieval system, or transmitted in any form or by any means – electronic, mechanical, photocopying, recording, or otherwise – without prior written permission from Apa Publications.

Contact us
Every effort has been made to ensure that this publication is accurate, free from safety risks, and provides accurate information. However, changes and errors are inevitable. The publisher is not responsible for any resulting loss, inconvenience, injury or safety concerns arising from the use of this book. If you notice any errors, outdated information, or potential safety risks, please send your comments with the subject line "Rough Guide Mini Rome Update" to mail@uk.roughguides.com.